THE NEW AFRICAN AMERICAN MAN

To: Al
Thank you for your
support —

Please enjoy this Book
as you travel on the
Road to Empowerment.

Peace & Empowerment,

Mitchell

4/28/03

THE NEW AFRICAN AMERICAN MAN
GUIDE TO SELF-EMPOWERMENT

BY

MALCOLM KELLY

BYE PUBLISHING SERVICES
OAKLAND, CALIFORNIA

For information address:
BYE Publishing Services
436 14th Street, Suite 727
Oakland, CA 94612
1-888-BYE-0101

Library of Congress Catalog Card Number: 96-95109

ISBN 0-9656739-0-1

A SELF-EMPOWERMENT BOOK
Printed in The United States of America

DEDICATION

I dedicate this book to the intuitive power of human creation.

ACKNOWLEDGMENTS

There are several people who played very important roles in the development of this book. I acknowledge the invaluable contributions of Lujuan Thompson, who acted as my editor during the various stages of writing. She continuously encouraged me to explain my ideas of empowerment in plain and simple language. She accomplished this with a keen editorial eye.

I also acknowledge the suggestions and feedback received from Vivian Gray, Thomas "Tom" Hawkins, and Jim Guy. I am deeply indebted to Rosalyn Robinson for typing and formatting the manuscript, and for having the patience to work with a new writer.

I give special thanks and acknowledgment to my wife, Carolyn. She encouraged me during moments of great turmoil to write and live the words of empowerment.

TABLE OF CONTENTS

INTRODUCTION

My name is Malcolm Kelly, aka "slave," "coon," "nigger," "darkie," "colored," "Negro," "black," and "African American." My introduction is not important nor is my name or the names given me by society. What I am attempting to do is describe, in a limited, pictorial sense, the process of development whereby one changes from a victim to an empowered person.

I am a man who has an asterisk beside all my accomplishments. Because of my color, society refuses to recognize me as a legitimate man. I live in a country where the views of the majority, in this case European Americans, take precedence over my views. Society considers me a victim of race and color.

I have spent most of my life trying to change society's view of me and to find an acceptable forum to present my ideas, which are as legitimate as those held by European Americans. The effects of trying are showing on my body and soul. However, I must continue to pursue empowerment because I know it is the only freedom that I will ever have in this society.

One of the most difficult decisions that each of us must make in life is to stand in our truth and listen to our inner voice of intuition. The majority of us are victims of the "follow the crowd" philosophy and find it very difficult to change or communicate our true thoughts to another person. Unfortunately, we are products of our environments, as each person is a composite of controlled and camouflaged emotions. We seldom express our true feelings to another person.

Even as I write this book, I find it difficult to express my true feelings. The difficulty is not whether I should tell the truth, but that my true thoughts are diametrically opposed to society's views of African Americans. Many people, black and white, may choose to focus on my feelings rather than the content of what I am saying.⁊ Typically, society labels a reliance on intuition as being radical.⌡ But the freedom I seek is greater than the judgments of this society.

So, with the guidance of the spirit within, I write this book to share with you a different meaning of empowerment. I remind you how to achieve freedom by using the principles of empowerment, which were available in the world even when the slaves felt they had to ask God and the European-American slave owner for their freedom. The same principles are available today for use at any time and at any place. [Anyone] who reads this book can use these principles to tap innate reservoirs of knowledge and to experience freedom now. I introduce a formula for removing layers of ignorance, which exist in the consciousness of anyone who is conditioned and restricted as a result of being born an African American.

This is not your standard motivational book. It is a story of how a young boy took images of those around him to form a vision of himself as a man. The story tells how as a man he began to use intuition to form another vision of himself as being empowered. Each chapter takes you a step closer to understanding your innate abilities and feeling empowered to exercise the freedom you have right now. Once you are introduced to the concepts, you can use them to stimulate your intuitive consciousness to action.

Each chapter connects with your intuitive mind and unleashes the power of knowing, held prisoner for so long by rational consciousness. The stimulated intuitive mind seeks the knowledge of empowerment and thus obtains dominance over the senses. When this occurs, you are entering the realm of pure freedom.

True empowerment is the unequivocal acceptance of the principles that govern intuition with the same or greater degree of confidence with which you accept the principles that govern language,

12

mathematics, and science. When you are truly empowered, you rely on intuition to make decisions about life, or to cope with life's deprivation, limitations, struggles and self-doubts to establish new personal beliefs and values. However, to achieve this level of awareness, you must first transcend, that is, lose the rational logical self which relies on language and logic, and find the non-rational intuitive-consciousness self.

The essence of this philosophy is based on the firm certainty that intuitive consciousness knows the truth about all things and is able to make infallible decisions. However, you must be trained to use intuition, just as children are taught to use language to express feelings about themselves and others.

My journey on the road to empowerment began during a speech which I gave in Las Vegas in 1990 to the National Black Federal Aviation Employees. This speech marked the beginning of my foray into the mysteries surrounding intuition.

When I wrote the Las Vegas speech, I was preoccupied with questions regarding whether I should stay within society's generally accepted subjects: integration, equality, and similar popular themes. I also questioned whether the racially diverse audience would respond favorably to a speech titled: "The Empowerment of African Americans — a vision for the '90s."

I pondered these questions primarily because in 1990 African American economic empowerment was not a popular subject among the ostensibly black intelligentsia who were still gung ho about pursuing political empowerment. African Americans used the decade of the '80s to focus on organizing the black vote, as Jesse Jackson ran for president, and many other African Americans won office as members of Congress, mayors and governor. Naturally, the community wanted to see the fruits of their labor manifested in increasing socio-political mobility.

Nonetheless, I chose the topic of empowerment, and when I finished the speech, several people in the audience came forward to talk with me. Some said while empowerment sounded good, they had concerns about what would happen if they and other blacks rejected the current political agenda. They believed that changing strategies at that point would undo all the hard work of registering voters and inspiring blacks to participate in the political process.

A few other people said they believed whites would interpret the empowerment of African Americans to be a philosophy of black separatism. (Black separatism represents the belief that blacks should not only have control over their lives and community, but that blacks should separate from the mainstream system.) Still others in my audience suggested that my concept of empowerment was unrealistic. They believed political empowerment was the most appropriate for blacks.

During the past several years, I have given similar speeches to ethnically diverse audiences around the country, and each time I receive different comments on what empowerment means. For example, during the Q&A session of one speech, a college student suggested that empowerment meant: "Blacks being in power and controlling the system." According to him, once blacks were in power, they could build, own, and manage major hotels, airlines, computer companies, supermarkets, banks, commercial insurance companies, and numerous other businesses.

This student was confusing empowerment with being in power. To him, change could occur only when African Americans successfully gained control of the American system. However, the philosophy of empowerment that I promote does not involve an exchange of power from one race to another, as much as it is based on one's way of being in the world. Once the perspective changes, skin color becomes irrelevant.

I am very cognizant of the fact that the word *empowerment,* now being widely used by the general American public, has several different meanings. Most notably, politicians freely refer to empowerment when addressing people who have indicated dissatisfaction with the status quo and make promises to empower them to achieve the desired changes.

Some ethnic groups, such as African Americans, use the word empowerment as a catalyst to gain public support for programs aimed at racial equality. To these groups, empowerment means the power to enjoy all the benefits European Americans enjoy. I could add to these examples of empowerment ad nauseam, and still not derive a true understanding of its basic philosophy as outlined in this book. For that, we must start with ourselves.

According to some western philosophers, the child begins his or her learning process with a blank mind (a "tabular rasa") and is taught language to describe all the human experiences and emotions. However, from an empowerment perspective, a child starts life with an empowered mind and must learn to use intuitive knowing on a level equal to or greater than rational knowing. The intuitive child is not a tabular rasa; this child is learning to reformulate information that he or she already knows.

Let's imagine that before entering the world as a human you are pure intuitive consciousness. In this state of consciousness you clearly know the reason for your birth. You know what purpose you are here to fulfill. You have appropriated the perfect body, mind, skin color, place of birth, and social status necessary to achieve your purpose. However, you also know and agree to abide by the laws that govern human birth. One of the primary laws is that intuitive-consciousness

15

initially loses its power to express in direct proportion to the gravitational pull of external conditions. While you might have been born to teach the world how to cure cancer, AIDS, or some other pernicious disease, your knowledge of truth is subordinated to the power of the senses in a world governed by appearances.

Let's further imagine that during infancy you attempt to impart this prenatal knowledge by speaking, and your sounds are interpreted by other humans as baby talk. The laws of creation have rendered you powerless to function without assistance from other people. You must be taught by humans to express yourself using the sounds and symbols of your native environment. In order for you to accomplish this task, (you are assigned human "guides" (parents, relatives, teachers, and so on) to sponsor your sensory development.) The guides who teach according to the blank mind theory interpret all your baby talk as requests for food, change of clothes, illness, temperature discomfort, and other things endemic to the needs of a baby. They ignore that you came here with knowledge.

The world, as represented by your guides, invokes prior claim to all your human rights to determine your needs, including what you are required to learn to become a successful person. Once you become part of the world society you are trained exclusively to use the ideas and experiences of others to make decisions about your life. It matters very little that you have a wealth of information from the "other world." Your guides have already decided your mind is blank. So when you point your finger at your first tree and smile as an acknowledgment that you really know the tree and its purpose, the guides simply interpret your sounds and expressions as being cute and babylike.

In due time, they will teach you that the thing you are pointing at is a tree. In the future, you will have increasingly more questions. Each time you go outside yourself for answers, you subordinate your

16

intuitive consciousness to the demand of rational consciousness. You diminish its powers — its sense of knowing. You lose the knowledge of your empowerment and cannot reclaim it again without transcending rational beliefs. Future questions will continue to occur until you give up the tendency to rely on the guides' interpretation of the world.

When we are very young, we test the truthfulness of the guides with constant questions: Who am I? Who are my parents? Am I adopted? What do I want to be when I become an adult? Why am I not a success like others? Your guides reaffirm your name and how you came into the world. They reaffirm that you will grow to become a successful person. Guides give you answers based on their observances of you since your birth, but these are colored by how they have chosen to live out their existence in the world.

As we know from our own childhoods, it is quite common for young children to observe others and to decide they best represent what we want to do in life. One day the child may say, "I want to be a doctor!" Several weeks later, the same child will exclaim, "I want to be a policeman," or a lawyer, a fireman or an airline pilot. Children frequently make these types of declarations to assist themselves in formulating future goals. Once they later select and accept one as a career goal,(then future success is measured by the level of achievement attained in the profession.)   ? ?

Some of you might find it easier to imagine your teenage years when you were constantly fighting with your parents for the rights to establish your identity, an identity separate and distinct from theirs. During these confrontations, your parents would tell you how their experiences, values, and dreams helped shape them into the people they are today. No doubt, while they were telling you about the old days, you were saying, "Fine! Fine! Fine! But I want to live my life differently from the way you lived yours."

Now try to recall how your parents reacted when you introduced them to something new and different from their accepted customs and beliefs. It did not matter to them whether you were wearing a new hairstyle and new clothes, using slang, or executing a new dance technique. (Their acceptance of differences was slow, cautious, and dependent upon whether large numbers of other parents were equally accepting.)

To escape from the world of the disempowered, adults must recapture that childlike self-assertion that comes from receiving and accepting intuitive knowing. In this respect, the philosophy of empowerment removes the layers of information that makes us disempowered. Thus, we begin the process of transcending logical reasoning to be empowered through use of our intuitive knowledge.

The process you use to transcend the logical consciousness can help you move beyond even the most difficult problems of life. Following are the primary concepts essential to understanding the philosophy of empowerment.

1. Vision. Form a clear vision of what you desire. Put aside your beliefs of lack, limitation, fear, worry, doubt, anger, revenge, personal avarice, and struggle. See only the end results of your accomplishments, and see them happening now in the present moment.

2. Embodiment. Once the vision is clearly defined and (accepted as existing in the present moment,)you must dare to act as if you are or have that which you have envisioned. Your embodiment must include the sum of the vision's parts without specifically defining them. For example, if your vision involves becoming a heart surgeon, then you must embody in the present moment all the attributes of a heart surgeon, even though you might be presently working as a medical technician or taxicab driver. Your embodiment of these attributes must be completely consistent with the vision and reflect how it can be manifested into the world.

3.   *Acceptance.* Stop relying solely on rational beliefs and trust intuition as the power that fertilizes and nurtures the vision to completion. This is the part of the empowerment process where you lose yourself (rational ideas) and find yourself (empowerment). This empowers you to transcend beliefs of fear, worry, lack, limitation, and struggle, which thwart the empowerment process by presenting themselves as unchangeable realities. In fact they are illusions in the necessary time interval between conception of an idea and its expression in the world.

4.   *Action.* Develop a daily action plan to overcome the fears and self-doubts, which accompanies most visions as they make their way through the necessary time interval. You must have disciplined and focused action in order for you to nurture your vision through the necessary time interval.

As I see it, once you have made the commitment to use the powers of intuition and created a clear vision of empowerment, you are on your way to discovering intuitive consciousness. Empowerment requires that you act from a position of knowing. If your vision is truly intuitive, it needs no assistance from others to manifest in the material world.

This book is to be used as a tool to stimulate the consciousness of those who seek a different way of life. The principles of empowerment are for all: those who see the injustice dealt to African Americans and others who are forced to live in dilapidated houses and neighborhoods riddled with crime and chemical dependency; those who understand that negativism, defeatism, and hopelessness are not the way to have a successful life; those who silently pray at night for God to keep their families safe from stray bullets; those who have positions of material power over others and believe these positions make them superior; those who use hate and ignorance as deterrents to love and knowledge; and those who are incarcerated in penal facilities, as well as those who are prisoners of dogma.

I suggest that while reading each chapter of this book that you try to imagine yourself doing all those wonderful things that you have never dared to approach because of all the reasons the world has given you for not doing them. I am confident that you will find the book an invaluable resource to help you recapture the vision of the time when you were empowered. With this goal in mind, I shall rest in knowing that you and I are one in intuitive consciousness.

PART I
OVERVIEW OF EMPOWERMENT

CHAPTER ONE
VISION OF EMPOWERMENT

In my vision I am limitless. Time is no longer a barrier,
consequently I see no obstacles or challenges. I am empowered.

Recently I had a vision that caused me to reexamine my life. I felt the need to assume control of my actions and direct them toward the goal I had set for achieving true empowerment. I used my mind to create an awareness of myself functioning as an empowered man with limitless power, confidence, money, health, skills, and the ability to use them. I was empowered to have everything I needed to manifest an idea into the world.

I saw no evidence of worry, fear, doubt, loneliness, or racism to prevent me from expressing myself in limitless forms. My vision of empowerment was completely free of lack, limitation, and struggle. I did not see myself in an imaginary heaven. I was living in Oakland, California, as a black man.

The vision displayed a wonderful sense of limitless power existing in my body. Nothing within me had changed except that I was using intuitive consciousness. I was able to create this vision based on a vivid dream where I discussed life's challenges with a wise old friend. Let me share with you what happened. Perhaps you can see the relevance to what you have experienced in your life.

In that dream, I was walking along a crowded street in Los Angeles, Oakland, or perhaps New York or Houston. I was unsure of the location, but I knew I was in the African-American part of town because the streets were filled with millions of African Americans. The buildings and stores reflected contemporary African-American aesthetics. People were walking frantically, trying to get away from this part of the city. They were moving toward mainstream society thinking they were on the road to prosperity. Thousands of people were stopping because of exhaustion, frustration, anger, confusion, and disbelief. But we who were determined to succeed kept on moving.

I was about midway in the group. I had no idea where I was going, but I felt assured that the people in front of me knew our destination. Wanting to expedite my trip to prosperity, I decided to apply my talents to move ahead of the people who were in my way. When they saw me pass, their faces revealed shock and disbelief that someone was leaving them behind. They accused me of trying to get ahead of the crowd at their expense. I felt good about leaving them and their envious minds behind. I did not realize that I too would experience the same envy when others passed me.

Along the way, we had a good view of a side street where we could see some travelers who had given up the long journey. They left the main road to pursue different lifestyles. This group became the topic of our conversations as we tried to move quickly away from them. However, their faces seemed to reflect contentment. I wanted very much to stop and talk with them. I wanted to ask why they decided to stop at this point of the journey rather than continue on to a better place. ⌐Like everyone else in the fast lane, I realized that if I stopped to talk I would lose my position in the group.⌐ Seeing small clusters of people scattered intermittently along the way, however, and being the curious soul that I am, I decided to stop and talk anyway.

"Hi!" I said to the couple standing in front of a well-kept house. "My name is Malcolm Kelly. I just got off the crowded road to ask why you decided to stay here rather than continuing on to the Great Society?"

The man extended his hand to shake mine. "My name is Carl and this is my wife Jackie," he replied with a smile. "Well suh, after traveling for so long and watching so many of our friends become causalities of the journey, my wife and I decided it was time to stop and put down our roots here. We were tired of trying to get to the other side of town."

His wife hardly waited for a pause before she started to elaborate. "Yes, dear," she interrupted. "I tell you, that is a mindless group of people traveling on the crowded road that you're on. Not one of them has any idea where they're going or what they'll find when they get there. They don't even know what kind of life they desire for themselves. Nearly everyone of them is so preoccupied with getting there that their minds are set to accept whatever conditions they find once they arrive."

She paused, then glanced toward the main road as if to punctuate her observation. "We heard about one African-American man," she said with a pensive expression, "who made it all the way to the Great Society and found it was controlled by whites. He said they live in big cities with tall office buildings; their neighborhoods have spacious houses. They eat in fancy restaurants and sleep in fancy hotels. Nearly all of them, except for some outcasts referred to as homeless, have lots of money. It is all they discuss in their meetings, conventions, homes, and churches."

"Yeah," Carl interrupted. "Somebody told me that once you get there and become a part of the society, you forget all the traveling you did. He told us you don't have to be with African Americans anymore, especially those who don't make it. We stopped because we didn't want to forget the millions of African American friends and traveling companions who were unwilling or unable to make it."

"Honey," Jackie quickly interrupted. "Don't forget to tell him what they told us about needing a password to get into the society."

"Yeah, I almost forgot," Carl chuckled. "The messengers who

came back from the society told us that if we didn't know the password, even after all the traveling, we still couldn't get in because we weren't white. They told us we had to change our African characteristics as much as possible. Our speech, dress, manners, culture, morals, ethics, loyalties, and thoughts had to become like European Americans."

"What's so wrong about that?" I asked. "I mean, they have so much money and material possessions, and those of us heading there have very little of either."

"Well, Malcolm," Carl replied, "there was another African-American man who got off the road as you did and never got back on again. He took a different path, then sent messengers back to tell us that we didn't have to spend our entire life traveling on that main road trying to reach the Great Society. We could stop anytime we liked and empower ourselves to build *our* society. So we decided to do that. As you can see, however, very few African Americans have joined us."

"You see Malcolm," Jackie interrupted, "we've been here in the battle zone trying to create a different society for ourselves and millions of other African-American travelers. But the messengers died without telling us how to get empowerment. They also didn't tell us what our society would look like after we created it. So we need someone willing to travel down that empty road over there — the road the empowerment messengers came from."

"We would take the trip ourselves," Carl said as he glanced at Jackie, "but we're too involved in our work here to assist others who desire a different life — a productive life for African Americans. By the way Malcolm, how do you feel about an empowered African-American society? Wait! Before you answer, we would like to ask you if you would be willing to travel down the road the other messengers came from, then come back and tell us what you see?"

I looked away at all my friends on the crowded road and then at Carl and Jackie. He had asked me a difficult question. At the moment, I desired to rejoin my friends. "First of all," I finally responded, "the reason I got off the road and gave up my position in line was because of curiosity and the desire to seek a different way. Many of us on the crowded road have heard from messengers who were talking about freedom for African Americans. These messengers gave us books to read about the great works of others who had traveled this same road. And, according to the information we received, when African Americans first entered the European-American society and received such cruel treatment, their pursuit of freedom became rooted in removing oppression rather than pursuing empowerment.

"Once, I asked one of the messengers why others hadn't succeeded in their fight for freedom. He said that by the time society lessened the physical oppression on the African Americans, many of them believed they were free, especially the ones who were able to live, work, and socialize with European Americans. They felt empowered enough to pressure the European Americans to lessen their oppression. Then they tried to get other African Americans to enter the same lifestyles."

"Malcolm, that's the same information we received from the messengers who came back from the front line," Carl exclaimed loudly.

"There's more, I said. "When the African Americans who had entered the European- American society worked to bring others into the mainstream, the European Americans said no. The leaders of their institutions stated unequivocally, in unison, that the masses of African Americans were not ready to enter into the society and would have to wait outside until their training, education, skills, and culture would allow them to socialize with European Americans."

"Did they tell you about how the blacks were fighting each other like crabs in a barrel?" Carl asked.

"Yes, they did," I replied. "They told us that even though we were moving ahead of many others on the road, we had to make sure we had all the things the European Americans wanted us to have. Otherwise we wouldn't be allowed to enter the main part of their society. (Those of us who believed our training, skills, and education would be sufficient to get us into the mainstream became frustrated, angry, and unsure of our life's purposes.) We began to seek other methods for achieving our definition of freedom, namely, empowerment."

"However," said Carl, "messengers who came from that lonely and empty road over there had been to the Great Society and told of having seen African Americans who were empowered."

"My friends and I heard rumors of an empowered African-American community, too," I agreed. "They said the people were not excluded from living, working, and developing themselves (to their highest level of human potential.) So I will go down the road the empowerment messengers traveled and I will send you information about what I see. Since it is such an empty-looking road, I would imagine that with my intellect, education, and training I should be able to move very quickly to its end. So both of you continue your work until I return."

Carl's face was a mask of happiness. "Malcolm, be sure to ask these questions," he said. "How did African Americans become victims? How should we use education to empower our children and ourselves? How can we overcome fear and worry? How can we recognize empowered African American leadership? How important is Christianity in helping us to become empowered people? How can we conquer loneliness, seek new friends, and achieve man-and womanhood?"

"Yes, Malcolm," Jackie said with a big smile, "also don't forget to ask, What is the concept of empowerment? How do we embody a vision of empowerment? How can we overcome our present conditions and achieve empowerment? How can we use failure and success to achieve empowerment? Why do we strive so hard for equality? How can empowerment help us to cope with racism? How can we move beyond alcohol and sexual myths to achieve harmonious relationships between males and females?"

"Okay guys," I said, "I'll do my best to get the answers, provided that they can be found on such a lonely road. Anyway, it was my pleasure to meet both of you and I hope the day will come when you will find the empowerment you are seeking."

As I walked away from Carl and Jackie, I felt a tremendous surge of fear mixed with worry, doubt, and loneliness. Quite frankly, it was because I was leaving the safety of the numbers and moving toward a new goal — a new vision of empowerment.

Once I entered the road, I was alone. There were no material or psychological support systems. Nor was there evidence of material comforts to support my beliefs that freedom and assimilation into the society were all one could hope to live for. I walked in darkness for a long time, unable to escape the feeling of doubt. I began questioning why I had left my safe and secure environment for the lonely and obscure life that I was now living on this dark, shapeless, and void road. At least on Main Street I could talk with others and be reassured that the people ahead of me had already come this way. I could feel secure within the crowd.

One day, or perhaps it was a night (I am unsure of the time because on the dark road time became irrelevant), I came upon an old African-American man. "Sir! Why are you on this lonely road by yourself?" I asked with a tinge of anxiety.

"Where are all the other empowered African Americans that are supposed to be traveling here?"

The man, whose name was Sage, said, "Young man, loneliness is a state of consciousness. That is one of the first things one examines on the road to empowerment. To be lonely is to experience all the things that control how we perceive ourselves. To be free, one must first become lonely by walking down a dark and empty road. "There are many people farther down the road and each one of them had to overcome the loneliness and doubt that you are presently feeling Others get off the road quickly. They come with questions about life in the world of appearances. After reaching me and spending some time examining their lives, some become afraid to go farther. They simply go back to Main Street.

"So before we continue any further, I need to know your name and what answers you seek. Nearly everyone from the world of appearances wants clarification about the concept of empowerment. Am I correct in your case, too?"

I looked at him, with his chocolate skin and white hair, and replied, "Yes, you are! My name is Malcolm Kelly. I, too, would like some answers about empowerment that have evaded me and caused me a great deal of pain. Millions of African Americans believe empowerment is something that they seek outside of themselves rather than something to be nurtured within. Perhaps by listening to some of my experiences you will be able to gain a clearer understanding of why so many seek empowerment without ever realizing what it truly means.

"As you will see, my life clearly reflects the lives of many African Americans. The rational process I used to form images of myself as a man is the same process that caused me to become a victim of human ignorance. I embodied these images as being Godlike. And by doing so, I moved further away from my true empowered self. But, if I hadn't lived the way I did, I wouldn't be able to tell others about my life, and how I claimed my freedom."

"Malcolm, I understand you clearly," he replied. "Unfortunately, many of you are imprisoned in the barrel of victims and fail to understand. The first step to achieving empowerment is to create an intuitive vision. The second step is to embody your vision. These are the keys in the endless journey of life."

"Sage, can you tell me how to embody my vision of empowerment?" I asked. I took a few steps closer to him.

"Yes, I can," he answered with a smile. "I will become part of your thoughts as you travel through the dark regions of your mind. On this journey, you will feel alone, but you won't be. I'll be with you. So let's begin our journey."

Suggestions for Creating a Vision of Empowerment

1. Sit down in a comfortable seat and take several deep breaths.

2. Slowly close your eyes and imagine your thoughts as a living entity.

3. Use your thoughts and write a list of your most pressing problems on an imaginary sheet of paper.

4. Clearly envision each problem in its present form in your life. That is, as debts, unemployment, worry, fear, etc. Then place the list under your feet.

5. Next imagine yourself as a colorless, formless, and faceless being with limitless power. Command your thoughts to leave your body and rise to a point where you are able to see yourself separated from your body.

6. Now, slowly, command your thoughts to travel away from wherever you are, toward one of the oceans. Imagine yourself traveling over the ocean of time faster than the speed of light to the perfect place of happiness and pleasure.

7. When you reach this ideal spot, feel the realness of happiness and pleasure. Relax your thoughts for a few minutes, then move on to the next part of the journey.

8. Command your thoughts to travel into the time continuum of the past, present, and future. Imagine yourself as a young child with bountiful energy and endless dreams. Clearly envision these dreams, and see yourself free of mountainous debts, mortgages, unemployment, substance abuse, or other pressing problems.

9. Now it's time to imagine yourself as a formless, faceless and colorless being with the power to travel beyond your child awareness. Command yourself to travel into the time continuum of intuitive consciousness.

10. In this state of intuitive awareness, imagine yourself being a part of all there is. Envision yourself in a position to observe the world from an empowered perspective. And it's from this perspective that you observe something you would like to create and share with the world. Whatever it is, a cure for a destructive disease, a work of art, or something else, you desire to enter the world to express it

11. Now, with this idea indelibly etched in your thoughts, imagine yourself being born with the perfect body, color, and mind to effortlessly express this purpose.

12. Maintain this vision of empowerment in your thoughts on your return journey through the various stages of your life. Keep it in your thoughts as you travel back over the ocean of time and come back to your body.

13. Observe your body sitting in a purposeless state, unable to function without your instructions. Know with certainty that the body's sole purpose is to assist you in expressing your new purpose. This understanding is important to your empowerment.

14. Command your body to heal itself of any pain, lethargy or its propensity to weaken in the face of major problems (illusions) and accept defeat. Wait a few seconds, then slowly merge your thoughts with your body in a marriage of empowerment.

15. Now, slowly, open your eyes to the visible world with the knowledge that a new person has been born. Even though the world doesn't see him, you know he lives.

CHAPTER TWO
CONCEPT OF EMPOWERMENT

The conception of a thing is always less than the thing itself. However, the consciousness that created the conception is always greater than the conception.

I opened my eyes and saw Sage walking toward me. He smiled and said, "Malcolm, you must seek the concept of empowerment with a free consciousness, free of lack, limitation, and struggle. So before you begin your journey into the past, I'm going to reveal to you insights on how to recall and understand your victim beliefs. You will find this useful when you are ready to go beyond the time constraints of victimhood.".

This is what Sage told me:

One begins the journey on the road to empowerment just as one begins any journey — by taking the first step. Since we are initially responsible psychologically and physically for the first phase of the trip, then how well we prepare will determine the time required to reach our destination. Many people never travel without maps to indicate whether they are going in the right direction. If you are traveling from San Francisco to New York City, you use a map to follow the different highways connecting the two cities. These maps were created by someone who made the journey and documented the information about distance, landmarks, locations, and directions.

When you arrive in New York City, there will be signs and landmarks indicating that you have reached your destination. By accepting the validity of the maps, you are placing your faith and belief in the map's creator. And in doing so, you willingly entrust your life and the lives of your family to a stranger based on your belief in the accuracy of the maps.

On the road to empowerment, the maps are within the individual and the acceptance of their validity is based on the acceptance of the knowledge given by the intuitive self. [You learn to accept responsibility for your actions without abdicating your power to someone else.]

Conversely, if you pack a lot of doubt about the maps, then you may wander aimlessly after going only a short distance. If you pack a lot of hate toward European Americans and other people, then you will be slowed down by events perceived to be attributed to others, and you will stop to fight with them. If you pack a lot of religious dogma, you may become confused between what you have read and learned about religion and what your internal maps show you. If you pack a lot of jealousy, envy, and distrust, then you may become preoccupied with judgments about the validity of your directions. This will undoubtedly slow you down. If you pack lack, limitation, and bad luck, then you will see many signs and landmarks that will trouble you and cause you to panic. You'll begin to wonder if you are even on the right road. If you pack greed, exploitation, and special status, then you will only be able to travel a very short distance. You will pick up all the excess supplies left behind by others and become overwhelmed and weighted down after traveling a very short distance.[7] If you pack history, mathematics, logic, and science, the ultimate tools of knowledge, then you will stop and argue fervently when you hear something contrary to your knowledge base.

On the road to empowerment, we need several things: an open mind, a belief in the philosophy of empowerment, unwavering love, an acceptance that (an abundance of opportunities exists in the world,) and a vision of empowering the self to make infallible decisions. The steps we are about to take are the beginning, and you should take them freely. If you tire quickly, don't despair. Just dispense with some of your supplies (beliefs) and rejoin us on the journey. This is a journey to understand why victims have been unable to achieve empowerment.

The idea of true empowerment is one created in a consciousness that is free of all restrictions. The basis for this idea goes back further in time than all human civilizations. Anyone who has this consciousness does not limit their lineage to a past civilization. For example, a victim believes that by tracing his lineage to African and Egyptian civilizations he is, in fact, freeing himself from the European-American culture. This identification with ancient black Egyptians allows him to argue that the vision of empowerment is found in a different culture. To be a descendant of a king is believed to be far better than being a descendant of a slave. Freedom to him is having a history free of slavery and white domination. However, true empowerment is to conceive of yourself living beyond human civilization in a place and time free of human lack, limitation, and struggle. Anyone who can conceive of him-or herself living in such a state of being can create a vision of true empowerment. But in their daily living, most people attempt to create a vision of empowerment with lack, limitation, and struggle as the cornerstone. Any vision created from such consciousness is doomed to failure. Even though the world may perceive the person who created the vision as being empowered, the vision will lack the two essential qualities: abundance and limitlessness.

Visions created from lack, limitation, and struggle are normally associated with the life experiences of the person creating the vision. Most people create these visions by using mind-action techniques to consciously remove themselves from the problems interfering with their desire for empowerment. One common method is to imagine yourself sitting comfortably with the problems of lack (such as the lack of money, power, or status) and limitation (inability to manifest your vision of success into the world) all around you.

Now close your eyes and imagine yourself rising above all these problems. You are floating. You are free. Further imagine that you are floating back to a time when you were physically free of these problems. How far back did you go? Most people who try this experiment for the first time go back to a time when they were four or six years old. Few can remember their lives at three years or less.

We can all agree that a four-year-old child is free from the problems of lack of money, power and status. However, we also can agree that a four year old has the problem of limitation — the limited ability to express his/her ideas of empowerment in the world. No matter how far back in time you visualize yourself living as a human, you still see lack and limitation as your companions. Mind experiments such as this one cannot take you to a place free of these problems. They merely take you to a higher degree of confusion, which distorts the true concept of empowerment.

To illustrate this point further, imagine that you are living as the son of the most powerful king of a country. Your father is able to bestow on you all privileges and gifts possible. As the king's son you have men and women obeying all your requests for life's pleasures. Since these adults are obeying your requests, you naturally believe you are empowered to live from this perspective. You perceive the vision of becoming king to be greater than any vision your servants could ever hope to manifest. However, upon becoming king you realize that a king's power is dependent on having loyal servants. To be a king without servants is to be one without power. You realize that your vision of being a king was created from a consciousness filled with images of co-dependency on others. Consequently, your vision was dominated by lack and limitation rather than abundance and limitlessness.

In contrast, in my concept of empowerment I envision you living in a time before the creation of kings — a period when you were pure intuitive conscious— a formless, faceless, and colorless being with the powers to create an infinite number of life expressions. In this state of awareness, you know that you have always possessed limitless ideas and concepts of things not present anywhere else in this vast universe.

Whenever you tap into the powers of intuitive consciousness you are no longer a prisoner of lack, limitation and struggle. You no longer see color, slavery, and poverty as barriers to your abilities to create. The concept of true empowerment does not allow you to speak from a perspective of a black man, but from one of an empowered man. Whenever I speak of empowerment from a perspective of intuitive knowing, I fully realize that the consciousness conceiving is greater than the thing being conceived. For example, the people who conceptualized automobiles, televisions, airplanes, and facsimile machines were greater than the things created because the ideas of creation preceded the things created. From this perspective, we are greater than all our creations.

The idea of empowerment is always present in the consciousness of all who dare to use it. Anyone who desires to create an empowered life is free to do so at anytime. For example, in our country wracked with violence, racism, and greed, people who believe they are victims are free to claim their freedom. This even applies to black youth who have embodied images of themselves as powerless. However, most of these youths cannot form a vision of empowerment because they have internalized society's definition of them as losers. They, like their parents, find it difficult to claim their freedom in a society designed to prevent them from doing so. They find it difficult to develop a concept of empowerment and embody its attributes in the present, while denying the negative self-image created by the senses in response to environmental influences.

(Even those who desire empowerment often refuse to use it, so they sink deeper into despair and conflict with their true selves.) Empowerment has always been present in this world and other worlds. It is like nuclear energy or electricity, which appears in a time comfortable with its presence. (The choice to use it or not is given to each individual. Empowerment cannot be claimed until you tap into the powers of intuitive consciousness.)

Suggestions for Embodying a Vision of Empowerment

1. Accept your vision of empowerment in the present moment and embody it as part of your daily lifestyle.

2. Remove all self-doubts regarding the efficacy of intuition, and eschew the how-tos.

3. When problems (illusions) appear in your life, accept them as that which conceals your vision of empowerment.

4. Remain committed to your vision, regardless of the time duration between conception and expression.

5. Trust intuition to guide your thoughts to an existence beyond your awareness of being a victim.

PART II
EMOTIONAL BELIEFS

CHAPTER THREE
FEAR

Fear is a state of consciousness one uses to escape from doing something one desires to do.

Today, I must take the actions necessary to challenge my long-held beliefs and fears. "Sage!" I shouted in a loud voice. "You know, even before I begin my journey, I first must acknowledge my fear."

"I know," he said as he walked slowly away into the darkness of my thoughts.

Fear begins the moment *all my life* we accept the idea that the powers of rational consciousness are greater than those of intuitive consciousness. For most of us this happens during our early childhood. For example, as little children we have dreams of being killed; attacked by dogs, snakes, or spiders; and falling from high hills. Our parents must constantly reassure us that ghosts are unreal, and that it is safe to sleep in a room without lights turned on.

As we grow older, fear comes up whenever we desire to do something, and we are unsure of the results. Fear is what prevents us from taking the small steps necessary to lay a foundation for success in a chosen profession. Fear also is one of the major obstacles that prevents African Americans from being empowered. In order for us to trust intuitive knowing, we first must transcend our beliefs of fear.

As a young boy, I was terrified of a boy named Joe Louis who was close to my same age. Needless to say, Joe Louis, the boy, tried to live up to the reputation of his famous namesake, the professional boxing champion named Joe Louis. For some unknown reason he decided I had crossed him, and he had to beat me up. He sternly told me, "If I see you again without your mamma, I'm going to kick your butt!" The fear of Joe Louis kicking my butt interfered with my life to the point that I couldn't go anywhere alone. I was very cautious to ensure that wherever I went, adults would be present.

Quite coincidentally I was taking boxing lessons from my cousin. And, according to him, I was becoming a fairly good boxer. Like many other young kids learning to box, I had perfected my left jab, but I still had difficulties using both hands in a combination fashion. I threw punches like a "wash woman." It was a strange phenomenon to experience my self-confidence as a boxer (unafraid to put on the gloves with anyone my size) and at the same time know that once I left that boxing arena I was still afraid of Joe Louis.

One hot Sunday afternoon, after a long workout, I went to the movies with some friends. As usual, the movie theater was very dark and crowded, which pleased me to no end. However, fear was still with me. Without warning, as I was waiting in line to get my usual order of popcorn, candy, and a soda, I heard a familiar, ominous voice ring out: "I told you to never let me see you again without your mamma!"

The fear I felt just hearing Joe Louis's voice was enough to stop me from getting my refreshments. I ran out of the theater as fast as I could with Joe Louis in hot pursuit. Luckily, I was able to out run him and get to the police substation close by the movie theater. Breathless and overcome by fear, I pleaded with the policemen to help me by arresting a 12-year-old kid.

I explained to the policemen how Joe Louis had threatened to beat me up and how afraid I was that he would actually do it. With facial expressions alternating between seriousness and laughter, the policemen consoled me. ("At some point you're gonna have to face this boy," they said. "You can't go through life being afraid of everyone who threatens to beat you up.") Good

They continued their intended motivational talk for so long until

I almost, but not quite, decided to leave my sanctuary with them and take my chances with Joe Louis. Almost, however, is not the same as doing. So I elected to stay put, and listen a little longer. Knowing that Joe Louis watched and waited across the street, I was perfectly content to stall until he decided to give up and leave. Fortunately, after a few more minutes he left, and I left too, even though I didn't feel empowered or confident. My fear remained with me and continued to be my companion.

Weeks after the Sunday incident, I was just as terrified of Joe Louis as I was on the first day he threatened to beat me up. Even the great and intense fear experienced by a 12 year old was unable to stop life from continuing. The fear I faced didn't prevent me from playing sports, visiting with my friends, and doing all the social things that a 12-year-old boy does.

Several weeks later, while playing basketball with my friends, I came face to face with my fear: Joe Louis. Seemingly he came out of nowhere — threatening and bigger than life, even though he was shorter than I. My friends urged me to fight and gave me encouragement, while other boys encouraged Joe Louis to beat me up. I was cornered and had to make a decision. I chose to fight. In a moment of panic, I elected to challenge my fear rather than have my friends think of me as a coward.

Once I made the decision and we actually started fighting, I quickly realized he was no match for me in boxing or wrestling. I immediately became my old confident self and went on to punch him out, along with the fear he brought with him. Suddenly, I couldn't justify why I was so afraid of someone who could not beat me in a fight. But, as we shall discover later on, fear is not a monster or immovable object. It is something outside of ourselves that the mind gives great power and authority.

As adults we face so many fears that my experience with Joe Louis may seem like child's play. But fear, whether in the mind of a child or an adult, has the power to influence our actions. Fear has as many definitions as the people experiencing it. When we act as victims, then fear is as a state of consciousness we use to find an escape from doing something we desire to do. Fear prevents a person from taking the small steps necessary to travel on the road to empowerment. It causes us to doubt the existence of intuitive consciousness.

For those people who have traveled with fear for so long that all memories of empowerment are lost, fear is master and lord over their lives. It manifests in many different images, which form the foundation for our reliance on rational knowing. Some examples are:

1. Fear of losing.
2. Fear of peer ridicule.
3. Fear of success.
4. Fear of failure.
5. Fear of living.
6. Fear of dying.
7. Fear of rejection.

I am reminded constantly by new age thinkers, psychologists and religious leaders (that the experiences of childhood become part of the makeup of the adult.) While I may not have had many Joe Louis-type events in my life, I, like most adults, still have had my full share of fears.

(Fear was an obstacle at each epoch of change and transition in my life.) Every change required me to confront fear regardless of the societal importance of the decision. I was afraid to leave home, get married, change jobs, and have children. I was afraid to join and to leave the Air Force. And my most recent fears surfaced when I started a business.

For an entrepreneur, starting a business involves totally conquering some fears and unleashing many others. Some of the most salient fears confronting the entrepreneur include:

1. Fear of losing money.
2. Fear of failure.
3. Fear of success.
4. Fear that one's skills are inadequate.
5. Fear of competition.
6. Fear of loss of security.
7. Fear of not having fringe benefits.
8. Fear of accepting responsibilities for one's decisions.

Initially, all of these fears act as adversaries rather than allies to those who thirst for economic self-sufficiency. (And because of fears we limit our capabilities to expand our businesses to reach their potential. We limit our vision of empowerment.) When we use fear as an ally, however, (we begin to accept challenges and take risks in our pursuit of empowerment.) We stir the action, which lifts us to levels never before achieved.

When I first started my business, I was not preoccupied with these common fears because I was not very serious about succeeding. My primary reason for undertaking a business venture was to have an income while I pursued what I believed would be a successful political career. Only when my political career did not succeed immediately, did I commit to making my business a success. Then I came face to face with all my fears.

At the outset, I was overwhelmed by the fear of asking a friend or stranger for assistance or business. (My fears caused me to involve my ego in all of my decisions and, in doing so, I personalized all of my rejections.) (My ego, while good and useful in many areas, was not my friend in the early stages of my business career.) I had a number of sleepless nights because the success I envisioned for myself was predicated on the public recognition of my achievements. My ego

49

needed a constant diet of praise such as: "There's Malcolm Kelly! He's a successful business man. Let's put him on all the VIP mailing lists."

It is things outside of ourselves that feed the fears, causing us to become paralyzed and afraid to take the actions necessary to accomplish our goals. These fears must be treated as responses to appearances outside of the body and mind. They achieve their importance based on the acceptance or rejection by the individual experiencing them. And — this is important— African Americans have been taught to give power to things outside of themselves. Consequently, those who control the environment and our lives through their power of definition have been able to diffuse our unity and purpose. We become paralyzed and afraid to take the actions necessary to accomplish our goals.

Our fear-based orientations to life came to us through our guides. My childhood curriculum included learning fear as a basis for achieving success. It was as if the adults in my life believed that giving children a constant diet of fear would develop people free of fear. Obviously, the opposite occurred. Their tools went beyond words and included a form of psychology rooted in pain and reward. Children quickly learned that adhering to the teachings of fear meant less pain, whereas, disregarding the teachings brought violence and pain.

With its elaborate use of punishment and reward to instill fear, slavery is a prime example of how the will to dominate controlled the will to be free. Perhaps more than anything else, fear caused the slaves to remain victims even after slavery was legally abolished. The fear of death caused "free" blacks to accept racial segregation rather than fight for complete freedom. Today, some young African-American males use fear tactics to intimidate blacks and seize control of the ghettos.

Fear is powerful when it manifests through humans. (The person who triggers fear in others is perceived to have an aura of huge proportions, as in the case of young gang members. A victim finds it hard to imagine that these seemingly fearless aggressors could ever become afraid of the same tactics they use on others.

The fears that historically have ruled our lives are still present in this generation that seeks empowerment. Fear of moving or beginning causes us to maintain the status quo, whether that may be slavery during one time, or segregation during another.

In this age of empowerment, we cannot allow fear to prevent us from creating new businesses, building new buildings, forging new alliances, entering new professions, developing new moral principles, and elevating and empowering the entire race. Most of all, we cannot allow fear to prevent us from challenging and competing with major corporations. The future belongs to those who can conquer their fears by using them as allies. Fear, after all, is just an extension of our imagination that has been blown out of proportion by our conditioned responses to life.

A few years ago, a woman told me, "Fear is dead and empowerment is alive." According to her, fear and empowerment cannot coexist. They draw their sustenance from each other; one comes into being at the expense of the other. I said to her that fear exists whenever someone has the desire to do something but is concerned about the consequences. Empowerment exists whenever someone has the desire to do something and knows that he or she has the power to create from a problem-free consciousness. Once you use intuitive conscious to create, fear is non-existent.

Suggestions for Overcoming Fear

1. Reaffirm your original vision of empowerment.

2. Imagine yourself functioning and living completely free of all fears in the present and future.

3. Act as if you are free of fears. Write a minimum of five things you can do to ensure that you maintain your freedom.

4. List at least five fears that constantly occur in your life: for example, fear of losing your job, wife, clothes, business, or life.

5. Identify the sources of your fears. Examine what causes you to believe that your present challenges cannot be removed. Exactly what do you anticipate happening if you take action to remove the fear?

6. Imagine the worst-case scenario and the best-case scenario. Which one has the greatest power in your life?

7. Remove the fears one at a time until their individual and collective powers are harmless to you. Challenge every fear with a positive action of empowerment. To do this requires that you deny the existence of the illusions created by the senses.

8. Go within yourself and use your intuition to make decisions. Continue to do this, even if your senses tell you that your actions do not make sense.

CHAPTER FOUR
WORRY

My face displays no worry because I have seen the face of empowerment, and it is mine.

Today my fears have been replaced by worry. I am like millions of other victims who begin their days worrying about illusions of lack, limitation, and struggle. I suppose if you tried hard enough you could imagine a worry-free society. The mere visualization would, undoubtedly, cause you to conclude that you were living in a utopian world, a place where you could enjoy peace of mind, where intentions and accomplishments could simply follow desire. However, before we can imagine a worry-free world, we might want to know how we achieve such a society. Is it possible to live in a material world and not worry about wealth? Does any of us truly believe a worry-free society will cause better results than the society achieved by worry?

To discern and reflect on a worry-free world requires only that you remember childhood experiences just before "do's" and "don'ts" took over your life. African-American children, with a legacy of slavery, are forced to cope with adult issues at an early age. We are required to discern, assimilate, and accept the multitude of emotions that normally are associated with adult behavior.

When I was a child, worry meant giving thought and concern to the material things that I wanted to possess. I fretted over whether I would get a new tricycle or a cap pistol for my birthday. When I was hungry and there was no food in the house, I worried about whether my mother would bring some food with her after finishing her work day. I worried about clothes every time I saw my friends in a new, stiffly starched pair of jeans or khaki pants. I worried when the rain weakened the old wood shingle roof and water began to leak through and wet our floors and beds.

Sometimes I worried not only about myself, but also about others whom I loved, like my mother.

Perhaps you can identify with this small child who, along with learning about other new things in the world, began to accept worry as a part of his life just as he was accepting happiness and love. (You will understand a little more about how worry prevents children from putting faith in their dreams of success.)

(Like it or not, who or what you are as an adult is the result of the seeds planted in you as a child.) The more you worried as a child, the more clouded your vision of empowerment will be when you become an adult. (The habits of worrying about things outside your control) are weed seeds that prevent you from eating the fruits of empowerment.

Today, there are millions of young victims living in the wretched material conditions of lack, limitation, and struggle in cities large and small throughout this country. Every day that the sun rises and sets, they are consumed by worry. If they are not worried about the essential items of food, clothing, and shelter, then they are worried about succumbing to the effects of drugs, crime, and unemployment. Or they may worry about how to change their conditions to become as they perceive European Americans to be, living a life of joy, abundance, and freedom from worry.

For the millions of victims born on American soil, society has created a hellhole — a well of negative emotions that grabs you whether you are on the bottom of the well or seeking actively to reach the top. At each level, whether ascending or descending, worry is omnipresent. (So the young victims who awakened this morning in racial ghettoes and penal institutions must find the inner strength to live another day.) This will be difficult to do because most of them worry simply about how to get off the bottom of the well, not how to achieve empowerment.

It has been widely quoted by many people that "When you are

on the bottom, there is no place to go but up." Well, when you live in government-owned housing projects and privately rented "shotgun shacks," (unless you empower yourself every day to move away from being a victim, you can still sink lower in the well.) The sheer pressure of so many people on the bottom pulls you down and keeps you there. Unless the hopelessness experienced by those on the bottom is replaced with empowerment, they will sink to an even lower level — so low, in fact, that a government-owned housing project apartment would appear to be as glamorous as a waterfront condominium.

We are on the bottom of this society simply because we have accepted society's ideas that we are inferior. This belief makes it almost impossible for us to discern the differences, if any, between a victim living in the projects and a victim living in an affluent community. Is the product of the projects consumed by worry while the person of affluence is not? I don't think so. Affluence and opulence do not remove worry from the consciousness of victims. (A change in environment and living conditions do not change a person's state of consciousness.)

The day slaves accepted that they were, in fact, slaves was the day they also began to worry about obtaining freedom. The same is true of being on the bottom of a well, located in the middle of a society that is defecating on you. All the debris discarded by those supposedly above you causes you to feel that your entire life must be devoted to reaching the top. Once a victim accepts the "bottom of the well consciousness," then all his waking moments are devoted to worrying about moving as far away from the bottom as he can get.

Worry is the state of non-empowered consciousness that becomes as much a part of a person as hair, brain, legs, and arms. (It is present whenever you desire to do something, but doubt your ability to do it.) For example, you interview for a new job and the interviewer tells you he will not make a decision until after all the applicants have been interviewed. He expects the entire process will take several weeks to complete. After the interview, you start to worry whether you were as qualified as the other applicants. You worry whether you said the right things during the interview. And, if you are black, you worry whether "they" are looking for an African American.

Empowerment, on the other hand, is beyond worry. Empowerment is connecting with the consciousness of knowing who you are, regardless of where your physical body happens to be. Being empowered will not remove you from physical conditions as much as it will create a state of consciousness which allows you to recognize that you possess the resources to change your living conditions. You have the power to override the tendency to worry.

To be an empowered person in a class/race conscious society such as the United States is to be lonely and seemingly unappreciated. Many of those at the bottom think that they can achieve success only by emulating the people who are several levels higher on the ladder. For example, I desperately wanted a college degree to help me obtain a management position in a company so I could boss around others. This desire gave power to the notion that the persons giving the orders were greater than the ones receiving them.

Meanwhile, like many other victim college students, I worried that I would not get off the bottom without obtaining the coveted college degree. Once I obtained it, however, I constantly worried about falling back to the bottom. My worry was not about how to use my college degree to accomplish my purpose in living; I was worried about being "better" than someone else. Unfortunately, society teaches you to emulate people who have achieved that which you seek.

The difference between empowered consciousness and non-empowered consciousness is as great as the difference between items perceived in darkness and ones perceived in light. The empowered person was taught to embrace worry, just as was the nonempowered victim. Similarly most people, victims and nonvictims alike, were taught many false statements about history that were accepted as truth, such as "Columbus discovered America" or "Greeks were the creators of philosophy."

We receive so much historical data designed to disempower us that when we hear its contrary, it sounds out of character. Whenever victims dispute the truthfulness of society's data they expect its response to be punitive. Society teaches people to accept the will of the majority. Those who dare to raise questions can expect their lives to become chaotic.

We have been taught to believe that when everything goes wrong in our lives we are on the verge of great change that will bring success. This may be a valid statement, but changes that occur in our lives when we are seeking to fulfill our purposes for being are never negative. It is not a matter of everything going wrong. We could say when our lives are in chaos, therein lies the potential to become very successful.

In another chapter of this book I argue that empowerment grows out of both success and failure. One could further add that success and failure are what cause you to worry, especially when you are seeking to leave the bottom of society.

Worry is what causes you to embrace doubt when you desire to accomplish something that you believe requires the involvement of another human being. I can worry about whether anyone will publish this book or whether anyone will read it or like it. However, for me to worry like this will not change the outcome. It is when I act from an empowered position that I can change the outcome. I can do this because worry is not present when I use the powers of intuitive knowing.

Worry is when you awake in the middle of the night unable to sleep because of some nagging problem. We are no more immune from worry's clutches in sleep than anywhere else. Recently, there have been nights (not as many as I had several years ago) when I just couldn't sleep. I was worried about not having adequate amounts of money, not having achieved the level of success that I desired, and my inability to change the physical and psychological oppression existing all around me.

Whenever I worry about having adequate money to do all the things I desire to do, I find that the worry is rooted in the ego-driven desire for success. I am worried about not having enough money because I desire a certain level of economic success. Or I desire to purchase some material goods to fulfill my desire to "keep up with the Jones."

During those late night moments when worry keeps me awake, I normally watch television or read a motivational book. Until recently, I rarely, if ever, did any work to accomplish my vision of empowerment. Some of my friends told me that they worried best late at night while eating a midnight snack or having a little "nightcap." According to them, eating or drinking moved their worries into the background until the next day. However, they failed to realize that worry never leaves for another day. It simply changes form and location.

Most of us have spent more of our lives with worry than without it. Once we make the commitment to travel on the road to empowerment, however, we must discard the emotion called worry. When we embrace empowerment consciousness, we enter what the "old black folks" called heaven.

In an empowered society, we do not start our day by worrying about food, clothing, shelter, and money. Our day begins with meditation, visualization, and a reaffirmation of our purpose. We control our destinies, whether we are living in the projects or anywhere else in the universe. This is the gift given to all of us by the Creator and Controller of the universe.

As I move down the road to empowerment, I worry less and express more and more definitive purpose. The old Sage told me that after worry had left me there would be many days when I would miss its presence and try to bring it back. In times of great challenge, out of habit, I may look for worry.

Suggestions for Overcoming Worry

1. Take the time to clearly define why you are worried. If you are worried about not having enough money, identify why you have the cash shortfall.

2. Reaffirm your vision of empowerment. Visualize yourself free of money worries.

3. Begin to take immediate action to achieve your vision. If you awaken in the middle of night, don't drink, eat, or watch television. Instead, reread your plans and write down at least five things you can do to earn the money you desire.

4. Create a vision of yourself with a hundred million dollars. Act as if you are already empowered with the money now. Ask: Would someone who possessed millions of dollars worry about five hundred dollars or, for that matter, one, ten or fifty thousand dollars? The answer reflects the level of your empowerment awareness. Do not dwell too much on the "how to," but on ensuring that your vision of empowerment is complete.

5. Go back to bed and rest peacefully, knowing that you are already wealthy and that through your actions the money you need will shortly be deposited into your bank account.

6. When you awaken in the morning, act as if you are the person you desire to become. Do this for several days and within a short time you will be totally free of worries about money.

7. You can apply these principles to any other problems (marriage, health, unemployment, and so on) that cause you to worry.

CHAPTER FIVE
FRIENDSHIP

A friend is someone who loves me and whose consciousness is empowered with love.

' As a six-year old boy, my thoughts were constantly changing with each new experience and each person who entered my life — added to my foundation for a successful life! I was, in effect, trading my parents' security blanket for a broader network that involved more people. Establishing friendships also meant becoming aware of the pressure and power of peer influences) These relationships became one of the most difficult barriers I had to transcend in order to obtain empowerment. When I first began this path, it was difficult to imagine friendships without peer influence, and almost impossible to imagine living without friends.

As a very young child my world consisted of few people my age. Most of my friends like Robert, Curtis, Leo, Charles, and Bobby were already in school. So when it was time for me to attend school to learn how to read, write, and count, I was not afraid to pursue a new venture.

On my first day of school, none of my friends were in class with me. I was in a room full of strangers. I was there to learn, among other things, how to live in the world with other kids my age. I entered the classroom and took a seat as near the back as possible. I sat quietly, patiently observing the other students, while looking for clues on what to do next.

The teacher, Miss Woods, also waited patiently for us to take our seats. As the bell rang, she moved from behind her desk, then went to the front of the class to stand opposite the blackboard. She was a tall, thin, light-complexioned woman with black wavy hair. I thought she was quite attractive and physically imposing. Primarily what I remember about her was the way she always chewed gum. Watching her chew gum awakened all the hunger pains in my little body, and I began to imagine what I would be eating for lunch long before lunch time.

Miss Woods began her introductions by saying her name and printing it on the blackboard. Since I didn't know how to write, I was amazed at how easily and quickly she could write her name. After introducing herself, she paused only long enough to catch her breath. "Before I call the class roll," she said, "I need to share with you some of the school's rules and policies. There will be no eating, chewing gum, drinking, talking without being asked to do so, playing around, or any other disruptive things that prevent me from teaching the class. Your failure to obey these rules will result in disciplinary action against the violators." In this case, disciplinary action meant spankings and/or using a ruler to rap our knuckles.

After giving us the rules, Miss Woods called the class roll alphabetically and said, "When you hear your name, stand and tell the class something about yourself." Each student stood when his or her name was called, said their names, the names of their parents or an older brother or sister. In some instances, they mentioned what profession they wanted to work in when they became adults. When it was my turn, I stood and repeated much of the same things the others had said and quickly sat down. By making my introduction, I felt a part of the class. I could now make new friends, though I had no idea who my new friends would be, since there were so many people to choose from.

I remember one boy, in particular, who seemed nervous like me during his introduction. I decided to introduce myself to him during our first recess and find out how he felt about being in school. I walked over to him and said, "Hi! My name is Malcolm Kelly. What's yours?"

"I'm Don!" he replied somewhat shyly with a startled look.

We shook hands, and I told him that I didn't like school and I was unhappy and scared.

"Hey man, I don't like it here myself," he responded. "There's nothing to do here that's fun."

After a brief discussion of our feelings, we decided that school was not a fun place to be, and we agreed to leave during the lunch period. So at eleven-thirty, we left school together and went to his house, since it was closer than mine. We agreed to tell his mother how scared and unhappy we were with school. We thought that if we could convince her, then we could use her to help us stay home.

We told his mother we didn't like school. We said there were just too many new kids for us to get used to, and it was very difficult to enjoy playing games with so many kids. We even complained about how the teacher wouldn't let us talk, play games, or change seats whenever we got the urge to do so. We tried to convince her that all we did in school was sit in our seats most of the time. And since we were bored with school, we wanted to stay home and play games with each other.

Needless to say, Don's mother gave us a pep talk about how she, too, had been afraid and unhappy on her first day of school. But after a few days she began to really enjoy it. She suggested that if we would just stay in school a few more days, we would find out that it was a real fun place to be. She told us this story with such sincerity that I believed it was true and I actually began to look forward to school being a "fun place."

Sure enough, after a few days I developed friendships with nearly everyone in my class. It seemed that nearly every day after school, I was telling my mother the name of a new friend. I bragged to her about all the fun things we did together and how we would be friends forever. I believed my new friends understood my thoughts, problems, challenges, and dreams better than any older person could. In fact, I placed so much importance on my new friendships that, in some instances, they seemed to be more important than my relationship with my mother.

After a while, my mother tired of hearing about every new kid being my best friend. One day she pointedly said, "Just because you meet someone and like them, don't make them your friends. You'll find out, if you're lucky, you may have only five people who you can truly call friends."

I heard my mother's words, but there was no way I could believe that when I became an adult I would have only five friends. I argued, at least to myself, about how many friends I had then, and surely when I got older I would have ten times as many. I considered my mother's definition of friendships to be old fashioned. I thought the differences between her friends and mine were like day and night; I believed mine would be with me whenever I needed them. It was difficult to think of obtaining happiness or success without them.

As I got older, my friendships became more complex. Friendships have a profound influence in shaping our ability to make decisions and cope with adult problems. Friends become like parents, requiring us to consider their feelings, desires, and opinions. As a teenager I needed a solid foundation to cope with sex and other issues. I now had to use different criteria to select friends who could help me cope with previously unknown problems. My relationships with high school friends required more commitment than that needed by a six year old.

My teenage friendships involved trust, integrity, support, love, understanding, and sharing. My friends and I agreed not to do cruel and harsh things to each other. We also agreed to acknowledge our rights to be selfish, especially in maintaining our bonds. Selfishness allowed us to declare "ownership" of another person similar to the manner in which we claimed our parents. So I was careful to develop friendships only with those teenagers who met my definition of what a friend should be.

It was essential for me to clearly define my relationships with both boys and girls. I hung out with the guys and plotted with them to get girls; however, we knew we could never date each other's girls if we were to remain friends. To do so meant we couldn't be trusted as friends. So no matter how fine my best friend's girl may have been, our friendship required that I treat her the way a brother treats his sister. I interacted with my best friend's girl as if she, too, were my best friend.

Granted, there were times when it was difficult to look at a sexually attractive girl and perceive her as a sister. There were several times in my life when sexual desires nearly overcame the commitment to friendship. I had to decide which was most important — the friendship or the sexual conquest.

When my friend Don and I became teenagers, he would constantly brag about going together with a particular girl who really liked him. Most of the time, the guys would simply dismiss Don's bragging as wishful thinking. We all knew the girl didn't really like him as a special boyfriend, but more as a brother. In fact, the girl told one of her friends that she liked me. So it created tension in our friendship every time Don bragged about the girl in my presence, even though I didn't like her as a special friend.

As fate would have it, one hot summer day my friend Shake asked me to go with him to his girlfriend's house to hang out for a while. I agreed reluctantly because Shake was dating the older sister of the girl Don liked. Although I didn't know if Don's friend would be at home, I prepared myself mentally to see her outside of Don's presence.

When we arrived, the older sister greeted us at the door and invited us in to meet their mother. After Shake and I talked with the mother for a few minutes, the girls invited us to sit with them in the living room. We had been talking and listening to music for an hour or so when Shake's girl suggested we go to the movies. Because the younger girl was very quiet, I had no idea of what she felt or thought about me going to the movies with them.

Shake looked at me inquisitively and asked, "Mac, is it all right with you?"

"Sure," I replied with a chuckle. "I don't mind going with you guys. By the way, what's the name of the movie you wanna see?"

"I can't remember the name, but it's a good movie starring William Holden and Jennifer Jones," the older sister replied with a loud laugh. (To this day I still cannot remember the name of the movie, "Love Is A Many Splendor Thing," without asking someone.)

At the theater there were only a few people in line because it was a noon matinee. We waited in the lobby for our popcorn, soft drinks, candy, and hot dogs, and I started feeling uncomfortable being with a girl who, supposedly, was dating a friend of mine. Rather than continue to feel uncomfortable and guilty, I asked her directly if she were dating Don.

"No!" she answered with an annoyed expression. "He likes me, but I don't like him in the same way. We're just friends, but he's not my special boyfriend or anything like that. To tell the truth, right now, I'm not going out with anyone special."

"Are you sure?" I asked.

Much to my regret, she simply said, "Yes."

We took our seats to watch the movie and began holding hands, kissing, and getting ourselves sexually overexcited. I really felt good. I was not in love or anything like that. I was simply happy. It was a good movie, while the conversation and kissing were just as good. Without realizing it at the time, I had experienced happiness with a female without engaging in sex. This gave me a different, but very pleasurable feeling of happiness.

Several weeks after our date, Don saw me at the Boys' Club and immediately confronted me. He walked over to me and said in a loud and angry voice, "Hey man, I don't appreciate you trying to hit on my old lady. I heard you took her to the movies. Kelly, I hope to tell you, man, I'm really pissed off. I thought you were my friend."

"She and I went to the movies together, but nothing heavy went down between us," I replied defensively. I also let him know that she said the two of them didn't have a serious relationship, and that she was free to go out with anyone she wanted.

Naturally, he didn't want to hear that, but I suspected at the time he knew the truth. He began calling me a traitor, a Judas. I didn't like him calling me that. "If you can't control your woman, then you don't deserve her," I responded angrily. "I've had enough of your shit, and if you want to get down over this, then let's get it on."

We walked toward each other to settle the matter with our fists. Before we could fight, however, several of the guys stopped us. After we sulked like little boys for an hour, a few of the guys asked us to join them in a game of basketball. Don and I were on the same team. We helped each other to make a couple of fantastic shots and suddenly we were laughing and bragging about our basketball abilities. He and I were friends again, and even today when I see him, he never fails to mention how I tried to "take his woman away from him."

The strategies we used to develop and maintain teenage

friendships are the same ones we use with adult friendships. We had a foundation for making judgments and decisions about potential friends based on whether they were liars, cheats, cruel, lacked integrity, or were incapable of supporting us, even when we were on the wrong side of a dispute. (Having principles is crucial to ensure that each person in the relationship is respected) Friends, like parents, teach us about living, interacting, and respecting the feelings of others. Friends offer suggestions and advice that is intended to help us. The advice is based on their perception of what they would do in a similar position. We learn to value their opinions so much that it doesn't matter that they may not have experience with the matter at hand.

When we decide to lift ourselves from our present condition, most of us actively solicit approval and advice from our friends. (We do so because guides have taught and trained us to seek advice and counsel from others before making big decisions in our lives) If we decide to quit a job, start a new business or attend college, it is highly likely that we will seek and accept advice from people who we believe have our highest good in mind. In most cases, these people are relatives and close friends.

Whenever I recall incidents where I solicited advice from some of my friends, I have to laugh aloud about the ludicrousness of it all. I was like the poor person seeking advice on how to change his life from someone else who is poor. It seems only natural that we would serve our highest good by seeking advice from someone who was materially rich. At least we would be seeking advice from someone who possessed what we desired to have.

Nevertheless, it is difficult to see outside the familiar. We want all the people close to us, family and friends, to go with us to the next level of awareness. However, it is nearly impossible to take others with us on the road to empowerment because each section on the road has it own guides.

(We meet new friends experienced in the level of consciousness that we seek to obtain, but who are not as dependent as we are) Before long, our dependence changes, too. As the Sage told me, "The farther you travel on the road, the less you depend on others for advice regarding decisions affecting life."

Even those friends experienced in using their intuitive knowledge are incapable of telling you what you need to do to fulfill your vision of empowerment. You seek advice from your inner being. Although it is not possible to avoid the inner conflict, when you shift your focus from one level of consciousness to another, your success depends solely on your ability to hear and to act upon your own counsel. There will be many days when your intuitive knowing will conflict with the desires of your rationally oriented family and friends. But as you change your center of focus from rational to intuitive consciousness, the nature of your relationships with family and friends also changes.

So when you make the decision to leave government-owned housing projects, drugs, alcohol, crime, a job or a belief system, rest peaceful in knowing, with certainty, that you cannot take parents and friends with you. You will meet new friends and you will develop a new support system of people experienced at the level of consciousness you are seeking to obtain. Once you achieve true empowerment, however, the only support you need is intuitive knowing.

Suggestions for Creating Empowered Friendships

1. List ten qualities you expect a friend to possess.

2. Describe the process you use to develop friendships.

3. Evaluate two of your previous friendships and describe why you became involved in them.

4. Refocus on your vision of empowerment and envision yourself connected to an infinite number of friends.

5. Redefine your friendships so that they are consistent with your vision of empowerment.

6. Compare your empowered friendships with your previous ones. Did you develop them for the same reasons?

7. Develop a list of ten empowered qualities you envision your friends possessing.

8. How many of the ten qualities do you possess?

CHAPTER SIX
SEX

Sex is a desire that I must constantly satisfy, but its pleasures can never satisfy my desire for love.

When I was a six-year-old first grader, not only didn't I know anything about arithmetic, writing, and spelling, I also didn't know anything about girls and sex. I believed the old adage that girls were "sugar and spice and everything nice." My guides described them as being "weaker than boys" and based on my training, I believed girls could not, or at least should not, be able to run, lift heavy objects, and wrestle like boys. However, there were a few exceptional six-year-old girls who could do all those things and many others better than my male friends and me. According to the guides, those girls were "tom boys."

My friends and I believed they were not really girls in the strictest sense, and this confused us because it gave us two perceptions of girls. First, we thought girls were fragile and physically weaker than boys. Second, they were equal to us in physical strength. This caused conflict whenever I wanted to choose a girl to play on my baseball team. During these moments, I questioned whether the tom boys were not actually boys with long hair.

Seeing girls together with female guides reinforced my confusion about their sexual status. Fragile and petite girls who sat in public places such as Sunday School class with their legs open invoked an immediate response from the guides. "Girl," they would say, "close your legs and pull your dress down. You don't want some boy looking under your dress." In those similar situations involving tom boys, the guides would just casually comment, "That girl's wild, she likes to play with boys. Somebody needs to tell her she's not a boy."

Since I didn't know why the guides made those comments, I interpreted their words to mean the fragile girls had something between their legs that the tom boys didn't have. This caused considerable debate between my friends and me as we tried to determine what, if anything, made the girls different.

As time passed, we grew increasingly curious about what the girls had between their legs that the guides felt was so important that it had to be hidden from us. So whenever we happened to think about it, we would dare each other to arbitrarily pull up a girl's dress. In response to a dare, we would run up close behind a girl and pull up her dress to sneak a look at what she had on under it. We would run away laughing about how we accepted the dare, but in nearly all those instances, the girls would be upset and, in some cases, cry.

When the guides saw us pull up the girls' dresses, they would get visibly upset and threaten to whip our butts if they caught us doing it again. "It's not nice for little boys to pull up little girls' dresses," they said.

Occasionally, however, my friends and I continued to pull similar childlike pranks on some unexpecting girls whenever someone issued a dare. But rarely, if ever, would one of us pull a daring prank on a girl unless we were in a group. To do so, I suspect, was like playing baseball or football by one's self.

It would be several years after the first grade pranks before I actually saw a girl's privates. However, some of my friends who had sisters or female cousins told me that "it" didn't look anything like ours did. According to them, "it was a split with a small hole and had nothing hanging out." Wanting to be more grown up than the rest of us, some of my friends would try to describe the girl's private area in great detail. They would use their thumb and fingers to squeeze their chin together while exclaiming, "It looks just like this!"

When I learned that the girls' private areas were not, at least not to me, as good as ours, I was disappointed. From what I was told, they didn't appear to have much to hide, since nothing was hanging out. Everything was already hidden inside the split. Some older boys told us the girls were made that way because babies came out of the split. I considered that to be ludicrous because the guides had taught me that babies were delivered by storks.

I still couldn't understand why the girls' privates were more important than ours. I had to wait a few years; when understanding came through child sex while playing house with a girl who lived across the street from me.

I normally didn't enjoy playing with girls because they used dolls, dishes, and other "dumb" things to play games, but on this particular day it was raining. Since my friends and I couldn't go outside, I accepted Jean's invitation to play with her at her house. Jean volunteered to show me how to play house. She started by creating a makeshift house that included a kitchen with all her play dishes, a bedroom with blanket and pillow on the floor, and a living room, complete with chairs and tables. Jean constructed our house within the limits of her small bedroom. She told me we would use our imagination to do the rest.

"We have to be married," Jean said. "So I'll play the wife and you play the husband."

"Okay!" I agreed without giving it much thought, even though I still thought playing house was a dumb game.

Jean fixed my breakfast in the make-believe kitchen and told me it was time for me to leave for work so she could wash, iron, cook, sew, and clean the house. She told me to imagine myself leaving the house, going to work, and then returning home after a hard day. So I walked out of Jean's room into her living room, waited a few minutes for the day to end, and then returned into our makeshift house. Jean met me at the door. She kissed me on the cheek, "Did you have a good day at work?" she asked with a smile.

I looked perplexed. She told me to say yes. "Yes dear, I had a good day at work, and it was hard work, too," I responded with a silly expression to illustrate my discomfort. "However, dear, I brought home a lot of money for us to buy clothes, a car, food, and anything else we might need."

"Sit down, you tired man, and rest your feet a few minutes before we eat dinner," she said with an adult-like expression.

After sitting for a few minutes in one of the living room chairs, we left for the kitchen, which she had decorated with her play dishes. She turned to me and said, "I hope you like the dinner I fixed for you."

I nodded my head yes, and sat down at the table. We drank water and kool-aid from small cups and pretended we were eating steak, potatoes, cabbage, greens, cornbread, and sweet potato pie. We also pretended to talk and act as we had seen dining grownups act all our lives.

When dinner was over, Jean turned to me and said, "Now we will sit up and talk, then we'll listen to the radio before getting ready for bed. As you know, I have to get up early tomorrow to run some errands."

We talked, pretended to listen to the radio for a few minutes, and then left for the bedroom. Jean had decorated the bedroom area of the "house" by placing a large blanket and quilt on the floor with two pillows.

"Now what?" I asked nervously while looking at her and the makeshift bed.

"Take off your clothes and get in the bed," she replied with a smile.

"I'm not taking off my clothes unless you take yours off first," I responded grinning.

"You silly boy, don't you know that we have to take off our work clothes and put on our night gown and pajamas before going to bed?" she said with a chuckle. "So start taking off your pants and shirt. Put on your pajamas while I take off my dress and put on my night gown."

We took off everything, except our underpants, and got into the bed. "Now you have to get on top of me and put your thing into my thing," Jean said.

I got on top of her. Then she used her hands to move her underpants to the side. I saw the split and it looked just as the guys had described it to me. Jean took her fingers and spread open the split to expose the inside, which was red and funny looking. She helped me to put my thing inside the split. Then she encouraged me to move my body in a back and forth motion, which would be described to me several years later as doing the "dog hunch."

Sadly, neither Jean nor I had any idea about how to engage in sex and receive its appropriate pleasures. We were simply emulating her perceptions of what the grownups did when they were in bed together.

By the time I became a teenager, I believed sex was an essential part of any meaningful relationship with a girl. For me to engage in sexual intercourse with a girl meant she really liked me. My feelings toward her were meaningless, because I simply wanted to have sex with her and nothing else. Engaging in sexual intercourse with a girl did not mean that I really liked her.

Primarily, my friends and I used sex as a means to reinforce our beliefs that men were physically stronger than women. Our beliefs of sexual superiority were also reinforced by our experiences with girls who made a lot of noise during sexual intercourse. To us, noise meant the girls recognized and accepted their roles as subordinate sex partners and were telling us, based on the sounds, how well we were performing.

Like most teenage boys, my sexual drive was extremely high and it was difficult for me to distinguish between the sexual, emotional, and intellectual desires I had for girls. Fulfilling our sexual desires with numerous sexual conquests was more important to us than admitting we loved or cared about the girls. During this time, the more girls you had sex with, the greater your popularity would be among your friends and other girls. The guy who was having sex with several different girls was generally the envy of the guys who had no girls. Also, many boys believed that most girls wanted to be with sexually popular boys, as we thought they wanted the challenge of taking that boy away from another girl.

One of the "in" things to brag about among the guys was the ability to climax two or more times without losing an erection. Also, who could have sex for thirty minutes or longer without stopping. We were more concerned about our sexual status among peers than trying to understand the many other different ways to develop a healthy emotional relationship with a girl. Unfortunately, we were born of a generation of males who were taught by their guides to perpetuate unequal sexual relationships with girls. We also were getting most of our sexual advice from older boys who were as sexually ignorant as we were.

Our definitions of male and female relationships were limited to myopic beliefs in male superiority. In fact, many teenagers were making decisions to marry each other based solely on the satisfaction of their sexual relationships. Many of the guys believed that if the girl was cute and sex with her was fulfilling, that was sufficient reason to develop a more permanent relationship. Teenagers who married did so to protect their sexual interests and to keep their relationships exclusive. Many teenagers thought sexual fulfillment represented true love between male and females.

There were tales of boys who used sex as the main deciding factor for their achieving manhood. Sex was the object of a relationship and we used our conquests to make statements about being men. A guy reached the pinnacle of male sexual prowess and manhood when two girls whom he was having sex with publicly fought for him. We thought such public encounters meant the boy was good in the sack. He was someone a younger boy could go to for advice about sexual relationships. But the fight also meant that the two girls' sexual status was at stake. One girl would be rejected if she was not as good sexually as the other, regardless of the outcome of the fight.

The sexual habits, beliefs, and experiences obtained by male teenagers — learned during a stage of sexual ignorance — are used to build future relationships with women: wives, girlfriends, and lovers. We believe these habits are time-proven methods for maintaining successful relationships.

Our society supports us because men have appropriated sex to mean power. Society places power in the penis. The bigger the male's penis, the greater his sexual power. The same formula for genital size is not used to give power to women, except when women appropriate it for themselves.

When we were young kids, we used a string to measure the sizes of our penises and compared them among ourselves, especially after having seen the penises of the older guys. It was important to us that one either had a long skinny penis, a long fat penis, or short and big in diameter. We constantly examined our penises to see whether they had increased in size since the last time we measured them. We continued this process until our penis had reached at least six inches long and three to four inches around. Once a person reached this size, he had power and peer respect.

One of the primary ideas behind our beliefs in the large penis syndrome is the notion that a large penis gave power to boys who were seeking instant manhood. Having a large penis also perpetuated the belief that women with small vaginas could be controlled and manipulated.

Some of us who engaged in early sex believed it was an act of power to witness the sounds of pain and pleasure emanating from girls as our penises opened up the small vagina to the world of male domination. Our preoccupation with penis size also served as false security and protection from other guys with smaller ones. Girls with large vaginas possessed power over all boys with small penises, although this power was not openly acknowledged. These boys were subconsciously reduced in power when they had sex with such girls. Often times, they would seek a girl with a smaller vagina to try to reestablish their power.

The whole issue of penis power is carried into adulthood. It is especially prominent when men judge women who are overtly independent to be acting like tom boys in need of a good screwing. Men who hold these beliefs interpret female independence as freedom from the control of the penis, and they believe independent women cannot reclaim their femininity until they willingly submit to male power. When men refer to women as bitches, whores, or some other derogatory name, the words reflect the "large penis syndrome." And if you ask these men why they make such remarks, most of them will probably say they are simply trying to bring women in check.

The problem is that many women accept traditional definitions of sexuality without question. They treat sex as a power originally belonging to men and believe women who desire the power must take it from them. A number of sociologists suggest that young women in the 1990s are seeking to redefine traditional sexual roles by transferring power from the penis to the vagina.

Some contemporary women engage freely in sex with several male partners without feeling the need to make a serious commitment. These women are not uncommonly the initiators in meeting and engaging in sex with men known to them only casually. I suspect they believe sexual freedom translates into power. They will undoubtedly discover, as men did, that there is little power in sexual conquests.

Some men trained in the standards of penis power are incapable of establishing healthy relationships with women unless they are willing to make a commitment to seek, embrace, and use the principles of empowerment. These principles are more concerned with the rational and intuitive consciousness that you need to have successful relationships than the power of sexual organs.

The principles of empowerment, if used properly, remove the ignorance that fuels beliefs in the power of the penis and vagina. An empowered individual recognizes sex as a natural human need that must be satisfied the same as one satisfies thirst and hunger. When you are thirsty, you do not try to drink all the water you see; when hungry, you do not try to eat all the foods on a menu. So too when using the principles of empowerment, you would not seek to have sex with everyone who is nearby when the need arises.

The empowered person recognizes sexual desires and needs, but does not become a prisoner of them. He or she is able to control the thoughts, emotions, and physical responses acquired at early stages of life which lead to sexual promiscuity and feelings of superiority.

True sexual fulfillment is found with acceptance and use of the principles of empowerment, and reaching a level of consciousness where relationships are based on respect for the total person and not just the parts: hands, legs, ears, penises, or vaginas.

Suggestions for Developing Empowered Sexual Beliefs

1. Describe three sexual beliefs that you acquired as a teenager.

2. Which one of these three beliefs is the most important to you now?

3. Describe your vision of an "ideal" sexual relationship.

4. Create a vision of empowerment and envision yourself as a colorless, formless, and faceless being.

5. As a colorless, formless, and faceless being, what are your requirements for an empowered sexual relationship?

6. Describe three new beliefs created from your vision of empowerment.

CHAPTER SEVEN
ALCOHOL

Alcohol provides an illusion of power, ambition, peace and courage.

Today I recognize the frailties of being a man. One of these frailties is alcohol abuse. Whenever I think about alcohol, I recall that most of us, at one time or another, drive pass liquor stores located in predominately African-American neighborhoods. We inevitably see black men standing in small groups, sitting in cars, and talking either in front of the store or in a nearby parking lot. Regardless of the time of day one drives by, these ubiquitous men are always present as a part of the store's motif.

Some of the economically privileged observers who see these black men hanging out during normal work hours might be compelled to judge their actions as the antithesis of society's work ethic. Some observers may also feel a sense of betrayal when they see these able-bodied, employable men simply hanging out and drinking alcohol all day. It is difficult to not judge them as society's failures. They represent everything we don't want to become. In fact, it's not uncommon for some to feel a sense of shame and embarrassment, especially when we are with European Americans and they see these men.

When I was a six-year-old first grader, I had a child's energy, enthusiasm, and inquisitiveness for people and life. I observed adults and older kids in the fourth, sixth, and eight grades and imagined myself being exactly like them when I reached their ages and sizes. I drew conclusions about others who were physically bigger and older than me without knowing anything about their private lives. I simply made a decision about my future life by looking at someone who represented a phase of life I had yet to achieve.

Nevertheless, these individuals possessed all the things I didn't have — size, muscles, and sufficient toughness to protect themselves from others. Occasionally I substituted academic intelligence for one of the attributes absent from my life. However, like most boys my age, my immediate ambition was to achieve a larger body. This would give me the strength to protect and provide for myself.

Whenever I thought about becoming a man, I looked outside of myself to know what that meant. In many instances, what I saw conflicted with the mainstream view of manhood. I saw many expressions of manhood; drinking alcohol and hanging out represented just one. The men who were drinking, hanging out at liquor stores, and teasing young kids who, like me, happened to pass by, always seemed to be enjoying themselves. They constantly engaged in loud, profane, aggressive, and yet innocuous conversations about sports, fights, women, and other adventures. Since they were adults (the people my mother instructed me to obey), I saw them as one of many examples that I could choose from on the way to becoming a man.

I studied their behavior and decided that one facet of being a man was drinking, hanging out, working occasionally or hustling, dancing and listening to music. I did not realize that these expressions of black manhood reflected the limited roles available to many black men at the time. I also did not see the men in these roles as abnormal. In fact, from my perspective, their lack of responsibility represented freedom, and that was what I prayed to have: to live anyway I chose. However, I also wanted the power and freedom to become a man like George Washington Carver, Ralph Bunche, or Booker T. Washington. Although I had not seen these men, I could use rational consciousness to understand that I had a choice.

I learned from those images of black men hanging out or working in positions substantially different from most European-American men, learning that was just as real as school. These images of what a man is supposed to be and do were impressed on my consciousness and nurtured there. They became the foundation that I used for making decisions about people and things in my life. The power of these images was reinforced by friends and parents at each development stage to ensure my ability to confidently discern when I became a man. Society's perception of my future was linked to the men hanging out. It was expected that as a black man, I would do no more than hang out on street corners. This was one of the lifestyles that American society associated with black males.

As I was growing up, it was considerably more natural to see black men as street corner drunks than to see them as bank officers or general managers of a large department store. When society's leaders saw black men hanging out, they apparently were not shocked enough to offer assistance in coping with the debilitating effects of alcohol. There are no historical data to show that the leaders created institutions to rehabilitate black alcoholics so they could become empowered.

Like it or not, those who are close to the young male child provide him with the most vivid role models. I wanted to be like my cousin Harold, who was six years older than me and treated me more like a brother than a cousin. Harold was big, strong, fast, and fearless. I was always impressed that whenever someone confronted him and tried to intimidate him, he never backed down. I enjoyed being around him to vicariously share his power, so I was constantly at his house.

One day I observed him and two friends planning to visit some girls on the other side of town. They were trying to get their stories together so that Harold's mother would believe they were going across town to do something else. While they were developing their strategy, I constantly interrupted them by asking if I could go too. My persistence brought angry responses. "Shut up! You're too young to hang out with us. Keep your little mouth shut before we kick your butt."

After considerable debate, they decided to tell Harold's mother that they were going to the west side of town to play baseball. That was my opening to join them, and I immediately took advantage of it. In the presence of Harold's mother, of course, I asked them to take me so I could learn to become a better baseball player.

"I wanna go," I pleaded. "Can I? Please take me with you! Please!"

Finally, Harold's mother said, "Y'all please take this screaming, loud-mouth boy with y'all. He's gotten on my last nerve, and the only way I'll let y'all go is if you take him."

So I tagged along. Harold and his friends waited until we were a few blocks from his house, before warning me not to tell his mother anything about what they really were going to do. If I did, they would kick my "little butt." I agreed to keep quiet. I would have agreed to almost anything just to go with them.

When we arrived at the park on the west side of town, several guys who lived in the neighborhood immediately confronted Harold and his friends. These guys said they came by to issue a little warning to leave their girls alone. A few angry words were exchanged between the groups regarding territorial rights. As the argument progressed, it became apparent that the guys didn't want to push Harold too far because of the reputation he had acquired for being tough.

Suddenly, I heard Harold tell the leader of the group not only would he "stomp a mud hole in his ass and walk it dry," but his little cousin would do the same to his little "sausage lips brother." I looked at the little kid called Sausage Lips who was about my age. I, too, had established a reputation as a good fighter, and Harold knew I wouldn't back down because I wanted to hang out with him. Harold and Sausage

Lips's brother brought us together directly opposite each other. They placed their right arms directly between our faces and said, "Whoever spits over our arms first is the baddest."

Well, I had enough experience in these types of situations to know that whoever spit first would spit directly in the other person's face. Sausage Lips and I stared at each other, made a few dares to see what the other would do, and suddenly, without warning, he smiled then spit on me. I immediately hit him with a right haymaker directly in his left eye. The fight was on. We fought hard until Harold and Sausage Lips's brother stopped us. Considering the comments made by the older guys, including Sausage Lips's brother, I emerged as winner. When Harold smiled and complimented me, I knew I had taken another step toward becoming a "man."

Several months after the fight, my friends and I were playing baseball in a park located almost directly in front of Harold's house. While we were choosing sides, we heard a woman's voice loudly scream, "Boy! What's wrong with you? I done told you 'bout trying to drink that rot gut whiskey."

We turned in the direction of the woman's voice and saw Harold running out his front door with his mother, stick in hand, in hot pursuit. Harold outran his mother and made it to the edge of his front lawn. Then he bent over and vomited in front of his mother, us, and anyone else who happened to be nearby.

Harold's mother repeated over and over again, "Boy, I done told you, you're not grown and shouldn't be trying to drink that bad whiskey. Don't you see how it's making you sick?"

Harold kept repeating, "I'm sorry, mamma. I promise ya I won't ever do this again."

My friends and I were laughing so loudly that we temporarily forgot who we were laughing at. Once Harold's reputation flashed into our minds, we left the park running. In spite of what happened to Harold, I still idolized him and wanted to grow up just like him. In my mind, I rationalized that Harold was sick because he was not quite 18 years old; if he kept drinking until he was 18, his stomach would become strong enough to handle the whiskey.

During the ensuing years, I saw many teenagers and adults trying to use alcohol to validate their manhood. The first time I had a drink of beer and took my first step toward manhood, I was fifteen years old. My friends and I got a few cans of beer and met behind the school to drink them. One of the guys passed the beer around to all of us and said, "Now, let me show you guys how to drink like a man." He opened the beer, took a big drink and said, "Ah! This really hits the spot."

I opened my first beer and took a drink. I didn't like the bitter taste, but since drinking alcohol symbolized one's manhood, I pretended to like it simply to impress my friends. I kept drinking the beer despite my body's warning rejections: nausea and dizziness. I continued to believe that the more I drank beer, the easier it would be for me to handle it. I also began drinking small amounts of whiskey and wine, and the effects escalated. The more I drank, the more my desire to drink increased. The more alcohol my friends and I drank, the more the older guys accepted us into the brotherhood of men.

Frequently, these guys bought the booze for us in exchange for "a little hit." They continuously egged us on to demonstrate our manhood by gulping large quantities of alcohol at one time. They would buy a half pint of whiskey or a fifth of wine (called a "short neck") and challenge us to drink the entire bottle. Like any misguided teenager trying to impress someone, I would try to drink the entire bottle without staggering or acting drunk. Staggering was a sure sign that I couldn't hold my liquor. My friends and I were unaware that by accepting theses challenges we were establishing a pattern of using alcohol more and more to validate our manhood.

Meanwhile, the ultimate opportunity to prove our ability to drink came with the senior prom. This was the occasion when we could drink and act like men. We had reached a level where the success of the prom depended solely on alcoholic and sexual conquests.

On the night of the prom, one of my friends borrowed a car from his parents. Before picking up our dates, we stopped to get a couple bottles of wine to "tidy us over" until we made it to the prom. We parked the car and drank the wine from plastic cups, which was a first for us. Normally we drank directly from the bottle.

We arrived at the home of one of the girls and rang the doorbell. Her father greeted us with a friendly smile and said, "You boys come on in. We've been expecting you."

By this time, however, we were so high it seemed our feet barely touched the ground as we glided into the house. I became conscious of the alcohol smell on my breath and began chewing gum and smoking cigarettes to try to mask the smell.

The girl's father escorted us to the kitchen where our three dates sat eating and talking with the girl's mother. Her mother smiled warmly and invited us to join them for a little snack. We politely thanked her, but told her we had eaten before leaving home. We chatted, but my mind was on getting my date and going to the prom. I had worked myself into a high level of anxiety by the time the girl's mother kissed her good-bye and instructed us to treat the girls like ladies. She also told us to bring them home at a respectful hour, and we assured her that we would take good care of them.

We left the house laughing and talking about how good it felt to be going to the prom. The day had finally arrived. The girls looked beautiful in different colored formal dresses and with their hair and makeup in place. My date looked exactly the way I had imagined as a child: a beautiful black Lena Horne. I wore black slacks, white formal coat, black bow-tie, black cummerbund, black shoes and socks, and sunglasses, to make me look really cool.

Before we could drive away, my date said, "I need to go back into the house and get my shoes."

The other girls left with her. I thought for a moment that it was strange because she was already wearing shoes. But the girls returned shortly with my date carrying a pair of ballerina-type shoes. (I learned later that the shoes were a safeguard, in case she had to walk back home.) She joined me on the back seat with my friend Chuck and his date. Peanut and his date sat in the front.

As we drove away, Peanut asked the girls if they wanted anything to drink. In unison they replied, "Yes." We stopped and bought gin, vodka, beer, sodas, ice, and cups. Then we drove aimlessly for a few minutes — talking, drinking, and trying to relax and enjoy what was a big night for all of us.

The alcohol had us feeling unsteady, talkative, and overconfident by the time we arrived at the school auditorium. I moved into the flow of this great social event. I went around the dance floor making sure that all my classmates knew I had arrived, which included dancing with my date and a few other girls. Most of the guys I talked with were drinking alcohol and kept it within easy reach. But this was not unusual since we drank to symbolize our manhood. My friends and I made periodic visits outside to have a quick drink of vodka, and we returned with our cups filled to share with our dates. We switched to vodka because the "old guys" claimed that it wouldn't leave an odor on your breath. But I had plenty of gum and mints to cover myself just in case this wasn't true.

For many years after the prom, whenever I attended social events,

I saw people using alcohol as a symbol of success and manhood. It didn't matter whether the event was a gala, military, community, or political affair, alcohol was always served. It was even sold to raise funds by some nonprofit organizations whose goal was to create positive community programs.

Nevertheless, from a personal perspective, drinking alcohol not only maintained my status as a man, it was an aid to help me cope with all the shit "the man" dumped on me every day. This new use of alcohol transcended my need to be a man and included other excuses and reasons for drinking, which became seemingly endless. Society's marketing of alcohol was as comprehensive as its marketing of Christianity. The stimulus was everywhere. Major companies marketed alcohol as a symbol of American manhood—obviously anyone could drink regardless of status, race, class, or gender. So every time I imagined having a good time socially, I thought of places where alcohol was served.

My belief that alcohol was an essential part of acceptable social behavior was reinforced each time I saw my supervisors, clients, and friends meeting at a bar for a drink. To me, the bar symbolized manhood; a place for men to unwind, blow off a little steam, and chase a few good-looking women. This behavior validated the relationship between alcohol and manhood. Without knowing it, I had added another layer of ignorance about true manhood.

Today, African-American boys have difficulty understanding manhood without positive outside intervention. The absence of black men in positions of authority adds to the dilemma confronting young black males. Unfortunately, they rely on alcohol to provide them with images of manhood, which they are unable to create with sober minds.

My experience with using alcohol as a measure of manhood is undoubtedly similar to many other African-American males. The images I had of black manhood came out of my anger, hurt, inferiority beliefs, and guilt. I was incapable of separating the every day rational reactions to life from the intuitive messages of my higher self. I couldn't envision myself as an empowered being. Instead, I saw a man who was a prisoner of his youth; a man who was a victim of outside influences; a man who was drinking alcohol to achieve and sustain his vision of manhood; a man in search of himself.

Drinking alcohol had become as much a part of my life as eating food. I never went without it for too long. Even as the level of consumption increased, however, I never considered myself an alcoholic. I suspect I didn't because everyone around me was drinking, and I didn't look and act like people described as alcoholics. They were the ones who drank outside liquor stores or displayed public drunkenness, and were incapable of functioning successfully in a job. I didn't fit this definition. I was able to work, attend college, and do many other things while drinking constantly. Alcohol did not imprison me. I was the image of success, when I drank I saw myself as being different from the bums who drank in cars or on street corners.

Nonetheless, I continued to drink alcohol throughout most of my life. The exact moment I made the commitment to seek empowerment was the moment when I realized that I couldn't achieve it and remain a prisoner of any substance outside of myself.

The more I embraced my intuitive knowing of the self as divine, the more conflict I experienced when a desire for alcohol arose. Knowing I had to choose one over the other, I chose empowerment. I simply stopped drinking alcohol in the same manner that I stopped drinking coffee, stopped worrying, and stopped being a victim.

I needed no help from outside sources such as counselors or therapists. My support came from realizing that before alcohol was created, I was empowered with all that I needed. I no longer felt the need to define manhood. I was free from the control of the erroneous symbols that described a man in conflict with the larger vision of himself. This vision needed no chemical substance to support or sustain it. I became a man at the exact moment when I clearly made the decision to embody the vision of empowerment. All actions taken thereafter were not about expressing manhood, but of simply empowering the self.

Needless to say, everyone who drinks alcohol desires to control it rather than admit to being its victim. However, those who desire the freedom of sobriety and empowerment must rely on intuition to guide them to the higher self. Unfortunately, the laws of human creation require that we rely on the teachings of others until we are able to balance the rational with intuitive knowing.

Whenever your beliefs about alcohol lead you beyond your present awareness of lack, limitation, and struggle, go within to a quiet place free of these images. Know that you have the power to manifest your highest potential. Rest in this place without giving any attention to alcohol, worry, guilt, blame, shame, or other illusions. It takes time to quiet the mind, but don't despair. To know that you have the power of an indivisible spirit coursing through your thoughts is to envision yourself empowered. Plant this vision in your mind as you leave this quiet place. As you begin to act on your vision, listen to the counsel of intuition and free yourself from the shackles of alcohol.

Suggestions for Overcoming Desires of Alcohol

1. Describe in detail the circumstances surrounding your life just prior to taking your very first drink of alcohol.

2. In this state of awareness, did you associate drinking alcohol with achieving manhood?

3. Describe three benefits you derived from drinking alcohol.

4. What was your purpose for drinking alcohol?

5. Describe your feelings regarding a loved one who abuses alcohol.

6. Reconnect with your vision of empowerment and envision your self as a faceless, colorless, and formless being. Is there a need for alcohol?

7. As a faceless, colorless, and formless being, are you able to envision your self free of desires of alcohol?

8. Describe your desires for alcohol while in a position of empowered awareness.

CHAPTER EIGHT
LONELINESS

I am lonely any time my consciousness feels detached from those things that I believe give me security.

Today I feel a deep sense of loneliness. It's the same feeling I had when I first entered the road to empowerment. Of all the emotions we must transcend to claim empowerment, loneliness is the most difficult. Judeo-Christian theologians claim that when God created man he realized that man was lonely, so he created woman as a companion. Since that time, most people know that when you are isolated for a long time, you will become lonely.

There are few places in America where you can stay long periods of time without seeing humans. Our prisons are especially crowded. When the warden really wants to punish someone, he orders him placed in solitary confinement away from the other prisoners. Some men have gone completely mad after spending a few days in solitary confinement, others claim they discovered God. In either case, when we are away from people, we begin to examine ourselves. Sometimes we like what we find, other times we don't. Solitude must first be experienced, however, before we can use our intuitive powers to transcend loneliness and achieve empowerment.

Some psychologists suggest that friendship is a solution to loneliness. Loneliness is also defined to mean someone who is without the physical presence of another person. As a child I don't recall experiencing loneliness because I was rarely alone. Parents, relatives, and friends were always around me during my formative years between one and six. Only once I separated from this small group of people did I experience loneliness.

Today, many people blame loneliness for all sorts of emotional and physical illnesses affecting the human mind and body. To counteract the power of loneliness, our guides encourage us to interact with as many people as possible. But I can recall numerous occasions when I have experienced loneliness while in a crowd of people. On those occasions, I found it difficult to define my feelings, perhaps because I was in the presence of people and things.

Loneliness has manifested its powers during different stages of my life. During the Vietnam War, I served in the Air Force and, like so many young men and women of my age, I got orders to go to South Vietnam. Vietnam felt like a stranger to me. My knowledge of the country was limited to TV and newspaper accounts that assaulted the entire American population. So I believed Vietnam meant needlessly killing and dying in a far away place. I wanted no part of either. But to fulfill my military commitment to my country, I accepted the assigned duty.

It was a hot mid-July day when I boarded the airplane with nearly 200 other military and civilian personnel. Seating assignments were made according to the time you checked-in and the first available seat you could find. I found an empty row and took the window seat.

I didn't feel happy, lonely, sad, or depressed; I simply was doing something I had to do. It was like taking castor oil for an upset stomach. The medicine is temporarily bitter to taste, but the effects are almost immediate and the taste becomes unimportant.

For the first hour or so I was quiet and lonely, even though two people were seated next to me and there were close to 200 people on the plane. Somewhere between California and Hawaii, I began a casual conversation with the guy sitting next to me. After we talked for a few minutes, another soldier sitting in the aisle seat joined our conversation by telling us how many times he had crossed the international date line. He said, "Once we reach the international date line, time will move forward one day. So if today is Thursday, when we cross the international date line, it will be Friday."

Since we anticipated crossing the date line sometime around midnight, by some strange mix-up in my head, I expected night would actually change to day. I interpreted an imaginary line to represent a physical change.

The plane ride to Vietnam was the longest one I had ever been on. We flew for so long that when I awoke from a short nap, I felt as if the plane was not moving at all. It definitely did not seem that we were traveling at a speed of 600 miles per hour.

After flying for nearly 15 hours, with short stops in Hawaii and Guam, we landed in the Philippine Islands at Clark Air Force Base. Military representatives from Clark met us at the air terminal, told us where to go, and confirmed that we would stay on the island approximately three days. They also told us where to take our original military files, which were to remain at Clark until we completed our tour of duty in Vietnam. I suspected that we also stopped at Clark to help us acclimate to the hot, humid weather, rest, and cope with jet lag.

On the way to my temporary housing, I received further instructions on where to report the next day. I had just unloaded my luggage when it suddenly started to rain very hard. The rain and wind were so heavy and strong I thought we were in a hurricane. When I looked out the barracks window, I couldn't see anything but rain — dense and powerful — all over the base.

A few minutes later, when I looked away from the rain, I found myself alone. All the other guys had checked-in and left. The rain and the strangeness of the country, stirred feelings of loneliness, homesickness, depression, and fear. Right in the midst of my thoughts, the rain stopped as abruptly as it had started. I immediately left to find the renowned airman's club, Coconut Grove. I had to meet and talk with someone just to assure myself that I wasn't alone. I needed other people to help me to feel secure and ease my loneliness. It didn't matter who they were.

I arrived at the Coconut Grove, looked around the cavernous building, and my spirits picked up. I saw people, and my thoughts turned to having a good time. I made a quick tour to check out the place, then headed straight to the bar. I ordered a double shot of bourbon on the rocks with a splash of water, then joined two "brothers" sitting at one of the many tables in the club.

I told them I had just arrived from the States and didn't have any idea where to go or what to do during my stay at Clark. One of them asked me where I had been stationed in the "world" (United States). He asked if I was going to 'Nam. I said, "I was stationed at Davis-Monthan in Tucson, Arizona, and I'm on my way to DaNang."

He started laughing, "Man, I don't envy you," he said. " 'Nam is a rough place to be. A lot of brothers are dying over there. I have friends all over Vietnam in places like Saigon, Bien Hoa, NaTrang, Pleiku, but not in DaNang. Brother, DaNang is close to North Vietnam. Man, you're right in the backyard of the VC."

We had several drinks and expanded our conversation about Vietnam to include the "world." Four other black airmen joined us. They were permanently stationed at Clark. These brothers said they knew what was happening and invited us to go into town with them. The town, Angeles, is several miles outside Clark.

We continued our drinks and conversation for another hour and left to board the Air Force bus for the short ride into town. The guys stationed at Clark showed us where to get off the bus. Only later would I understand the importance of knowing where to get off the bus. I looked around at all the nightclubs with names similar to those of clubs located in black areas of American cities. Masses of people, primarily African- American airmen, flowed in and out of clubs located on both sides of the street for several blocks. Soul music pulsated in the air. The nightclub atmosphere reminded me of Oakland California. ✗ We went barhopping through the clubs on one side of the street, then the other. In some cases, we stopped just to check out the club.

Finally, we selected a club that was crowded with men and women. We took a table and ordered drinks. Recent songs from the States filled the room. The brothers were doing the latest American dances with the Filipino hostesses. I was amazed to see the Filipino women dancing, talking, and acting like the sisters back home. We joined in the fun, dancing, drinking, and talking. I drank the local beer instead of my customary bourbon. This was a big mistake. After a couple of beers, I suddenly felt tired and sleepy. The long trip, the jet lag, and the alcohol were taking their toll on my body. I told the guys I needed to go outside and get some fresh air.

A couple of the guys left with me, saying, "It's not safe for a brother to walk the streets alone." While we walked, I saw a part of the street that I had not noticed before. Here the clubs had different names and the masses of people entering and leaving them were white. The brothers explained to me that the whites had their part of town and the blacks had theirs. I was shocked and disappointed to learn that racism had followed me halfway around the world. According to the brothers, if I had walked into the white part of town alone, I probably would have been attacked.

The walk cleared my head and I was able to check out a few other clubs before it was time to board the bus to go back to the air base. We boarded the bus in the same area that we left several hours ago. After picking up the brothers, the driver drove farther down the street to pick up the white airmen. On the bus, black and white airmen integrated again according to military policies. We could temporarily camouflage our dislikes for each other by pretending nothing was significant about the separated social policies practiced away from the air base. I wondered whether we would continue social segregation in Vietnam.

Nearly everyone on the bus had been drinking and wherever you find racism and drinking, trouble is not too far away. Sure enough, before we reached the base an argument erupted between a black airman and white airman. It was not serious, just loud talk and a need to lash out at each other. They made threats and counterthreats all the way to the base. The rest of us slept. By the time we arrived at the base, both of the arguing airmen were asleep.

I spent the next two days checking out the sights on the base. A day later, I boarded a plane for Saigon. Unlike the flight to the Philippines, this one took only four hours.

We landed in Saigon as the sun was going down. A group of military people greeted us at the airport. They provided information and instructions regarding our luggage, paper work, and temporary housing during our two-day stay. Those of us who were going to other bases in Vietnam were told to create a separate line. We were given additional instructions on travel.

On the way to our temporary living quarters, we discovered that home for the next couple of days would be a place the locals called Tent City, the largest group of tents anywhere in the world. As far as the eyes could see there was nothing but tents. I was assigned a tent which contained a bed enclosed by a mosquito net, two cans of insect spray, a wall locker, and foot locker.

I slowly put away my luggage, then looked around to see who else was in the place. I saw three brothers engaged in what appeared to be a casual conversation. I walked to the bed where they sat and introduced myself. "I just arrived here from the States," I said and extended my hand. "I'm trying to find out what to do around here for the next couple of days. Do you guys know where the airmen's club is located?"

One of the brothers said he, too, had just arrived from the States a few hours earlier and had no idea where anything was at this point. He went on to say how the three of them were just killing time until chow time, then they were going to scout the area for the happenings. The brother sitting on the footlocker interrupted him by saying, "I can tell you guys one thing, I'm gonna find the club, or some damn place because I need a cold beer to help me deal with this heat. Man, it's hot here."

I suggested that we eat dinner first, then ask someone at the mess hall to give us directions to the airmen's club. We all agreed and left for the mess hall to eat dinner. The mess hall was packed with hungry airmen. We asked one of the cooks serving the food for directions to the airmen's club. He gave us the directions and jokingly said he wished he was going with us. We ate dinner, chatted for a few minutes, and left for the club.

This club was small compared to the Coconut Grove club in the Philippines. However, I had to remember we were in the middle of a war zone. The club was packed with African-American airmen partying to the sounds of soul music. We looked around for seats and found an empty table near several brothers who were drinking and talking so loudly they could be heard above the music. The skimpily clad Vietnamese waitress came by and took my order for a bourbon on the rocks with a splash of water. (Later on, I would drink my drinks without water or ice because of the parasites found in the Vietnamese water.) The four of us from Tent City got our drinks and continued to talk about where we were going to be stationed. Two of the guys were staying in Saigon and the other one, Robby, was going to DaNang, where I was also headed. Robby and I immediately became fast friends.

Suddenly, a lively discussion at a nearby table caught my attention. One brother in particular seemed to dominate the discussion. He appeared to be very articulate, but was also visibly under the influence of alcohol, and quite possibly suffering from the stress and loneliness of living in Vietnam. We later learned from some of the other guys that this brother had spent a year in the jungles of 'Nam and was now on his way back to the "world." He talked endlessly about everything, though his conversation seemed disjointed and without purpose. He acted as if he had really lost it. Robby and I gave each other a perplexed look to convey the message: What's wrong with this dude? I sure hope I don't end up like him after a year in 'Nam.

We continued to party until early in the morning. I wanted to party until the next day because I was not too pleased with the living accommodations in Tent City. However, we left just before the club closed, and that brother was still drinking and ranting in the same manner. On our way back to Tent City, I made a pledge to myself not to allow the pressures of the war to reduce me to a disoriented man like the brother in the club. He became the symbol for what I did not want to become. I didn't want to return from 'Nam an alcoholic (though I was one already and didn't know it).

Two days later, after a lot of partying on base and in downtown Saigon, we boarded a C-123 airplane (nicknamed "Gooney Bird") for the relatively short flight to DaNang. Once we were airborne, my thoughts of how funny life can be replaced thoughts of war. Throughout my life, I had established lifelong happy relationships with people. I could always call or visit them when I was lonely and needed to talk with someone who knew all the things I liked and disliked. They were now safe in the States while I was riding a prop plane over the jungles of Vietnam. I was entering a new stage in my life and all those past relationships had to be replaced with people better suited to be with me during this stage. These new people would help me to overcome the loneliness caused by separation from friends and relatives.

In DaNang, we boarded the bus for the short ride to another Tent City. The sergeant riding with us assured us that we would only be in the tents until we were officially processed. Then we would be assigned permanent living quarters.

Sure enough, two days later, Robby and I received permanent living quarters in a suitably large barracks-type building. We also received a large wall locker, a footlocker, a bed with a mosquito net, and several cans of insect repellent. The building was fully occupied. I looked around and saw only the faces of African- American airmen. Most of them came by and introduced themselves to us. They had names like Brooks, Faulkner, Hawkins, Green, Ike, Northrop, Rogers, Brown, "Stump Davis," "Young Blood," "Big T from Baltimore," "Panama," and many others. And, as diverse as their names, were the cities and towns they came from in the States. Knowing your hometown was a big deal to the brothers in 'Nam. If they knew your hometown, then they could introduce you to your "homeboys" in the area. Ironically, there wasn't anyone black on base from either Oakland or Texas.

I asked a couple of the guys my usual questions: "Where's the action? Is there any excitement around this place?"

One of the brothers who had been in 'Nam for several months said, with a rapid fire voice, the names of all the clubs in downtown DaNang (a city of approximately 500,000) and the two clubs located on the air base. He also told me about a new form of entertainment the brothers called "blowing soul." I asked him to explain exactly what blowing soul meant.

He shook his head and said, "If you want to find out, you'll have to join us tonight behind the barracks. Then you'll get an answer."

After finishing work, I ate dinner in the mess hall and took a few minutes to unwind, then I picked-up Robby and we joined the other brothers headed to the back of the barracks. The airman named Faulkner turned on his portable record player and the soulful voice of Curtis Mayfield permeated the air. I turned around to see the other brothers bringing bottles of scotch, bourbon, gin, vodka, beer, sodas, and many other kinds of drinks. They said everyone would share. I also observed several guys who appeared to have high status with the group, and the others seemed to gravitate toward them. They weren't officers because we were all in the same rank. "Who are those brothers?" I asked one of the guys nearby.

"Just hold on, man," he replied and gave me the black power hand shake. "They'll tell you in a few minutes."

One of the guys in the group began by welcoming the newcomers to the war. He said there were certain rules the brothers had established to ensure that we conduct ourselves properly during our tour in 'Nam. Included in those rules was a pledge required of all the brothers. The pledge required one vow: "Never to physically fight or disrespect another brother during your tour in 'Nam. Failure to abide by this pledge would result in your immediate ostracism from the blowing soul sessions and other events such as barbecues, picnics, and parties sponsored by African-American airmen.

Robby and I took the pledge. It was the first time in my life that I had witnessed brothers coming together around our own best interest. It not only made me feel good, but also proud to be black. Once they welcomed Robby and me to the group, we were ready to blow soul.

To blow soul, you had to join in a free wheeling discussion with several other guys and take a leading part in the discussion. Once you entered the discussion, you had to contribute to it regardless of the subject matter or how many times it changed. Failure to do so simply meant you had to shut up and sit on the sidelines until you found a subject you were comfortable discussing. Obviously, once you were out, the people who remained would continue talking as long as possible about the subject you couldn't discuss.

Blowing soul was an art and an effective way to combat the feelings of loneliness, depression, and anger. I found this to be true during my first months in 'Nam. The first three months were the most difficult to cope with. We used the blowing soul sessions to help us handle difficult situations. For example, at lunch time one guy might ask if we wanted to get together later that night and blow some soul. Just the idea of having something to do after work gave me something to look forward to. I participated in nearly all the sessions.

After a few months of successfully blowing soul, I earned the nickname "Preach" from the brothers. Many of the guys stationed with me in 'Nam probably don't remember my correct name, but if you mention Preach, they will remember.

Blowing soul in 'Nam was one of the many tools I used to handle difficult situations. The loneliness I faced grew out of an insecure consciousness that required the constant presence of people and things for me to survive from one day to the next day. The brothers and I came together not to seek true empowerment, but to establish a system for temporary survival in the midst of our despair. We wanted something to help us cope with our loneliness.

By discussing loneliness through my Vietnam experiences, I am offering you a perspective of how I coped at one time in my life. Loneliness expresses a lack, often a desire to be with another person or in a different environment. For example, if your heart calls San Francisco home and you are living in Cleveland, Ohio, you will experience loneliness for San Francisco. You can probably find a similar example for your own personal relationships. Sometimes we try to overcome loneliness by seeking a physical change — different people or a different environment — but often we only exchange one set of problems for another.

People who feel separated from family, friends, houses, even automobiles, try to escape through seemingly rational actions. They move from one city to another, change partners in intimate relationships or rely on inanimate objects such as television, books and movies to provide a temporary sanctuary from loneliness. But these are all illusions. In fact, the problems people face when trying to avoid loneliness are more elusive than we realize.

Empowerment does not require that we physically give up all of our friends and family, and move to another city. Empowerment requires us to clearly establish a vision for fulfilling our purpose for living. Once you accomplish this task, friends and family will travel on the journey as far as their commitment to your vision will allow. You will not look at your situation with loneliness. Empowered by intuition, you will see and experience only freedom, even when you are alone.

Suddenly, Sage appeared. "Malcolm, I sense that you have gone far enough with examining your emotional beliefs," he said with a concerned expression. "As you know, this is the first stage of the empowerment process. We still have a long way to go."

"It may be the first stage, but I felt good acknowledging my feelings," I replied. "I would've never realized the impact my beliefs had in keeping me a victim."

"Yeah, I know," he replied with a smile. "Most victims are afraid to examine their beliefs. They are too busy trying to maintain them. Anyway, now we can move on and examine your societal beliefs. They are the ones responsible for your anger, self-hatred, and misguided actions."

Suggestions for Overcoming Beliefs of Loneliness

1. At what age did you become aware of feelings of loneliness?

2. Describe your feelings during this first experience.

3. What factors caused you to feel lonely?

4. How did you overcome this feeling?

5. Reconnect with your vision of empowerment and envision your self as a faceless, colorless, and formless being. Are you of aware of feelings of loneliness?

6. As a faceless, colorless, and formless being, what is your perception of loneliness?

7. What is the relationship between loneliness and your vision of empowerment?

8. Do you require people to assuage your feelings of loneliness?

PART III
SOCIETAL BELIEFS

CHAPTER NINE
LEADERSHIP

Leaders provide security for those persons who are lost and need someone to guide them to a safe place.

Today I must examine my beliefs about this society. I find it difficult to understand why victims rely on beliefs that designate other individuals as their leaders. When I was a young boy, the leaders among us were not appointed. People became leaders based on their skills, presence, determination, and courage. I believed I was a leader and I wanted very much to be a leader among my peers. My qualifications included excellent academic skills, great acting and oratory skills, a sense of humor, determination, and, in many instances, courage. Yet in spite of my desires and perceived skills, I could not get my peers to accept me in a true leadership role, at least when I was a child.

Initially, I wanted to be a leader so that I could have recognition, status, and power over other kids. I wanted others to admire me rather than look down on me. This was both an acknowledgment of my victim status and an opportunity for me to separate myself from other victims. However, like most victims, I also believed that leadership in the African-American community manifested whenever the economic, moral, and political conditions were in a state of depression and despair. Leaders come forth fully formed with leadership qualities, knowledge, vision, charisma, and timing. And in the African-American community, besieged by a lack of money, food, housing, education, success, and empowerment, people are always looking for a new leader.

This constant search for leadership has produced countless leaders who were not only victims, but unaware of the level of their victimization. They were nonempowered leaders. To understand the differences between nonempowered African-American leadership and empowered leadership, think of empowerment as a strategy of leadership that has not existed in the world before.

We define leadership as courage, vision, and action in spite of obstacles. The nonempowered leader addresses the conditions of deprivation and limitation faced by nonempowered people. The nonempowered leader acts on these issues whenever his or her followers feel the need for change. Since the conditions of deprivation and limitation look different in different time periods, the leaders have been unable to develop a focused, empowered agenda. Consequently, African-American leaders come and go within short periods of time without adequately addressing the real community needs. Some could argue that all leaders fit into this category, and perhaps this is a valid statement.

Young children become nonempowered leaders based on how well they satisfy the fears of their followers, or their knowledge of events, sports, movies, and toys. While growing up I had the opportunity to observe two distinct types of young men and to study the qualities that made them into leaders. The first, Bobby, exemplified the knowledge and courage necessary to command a small group of followers. He was a master at holding court, a term appropriately defined as dominating lengthy conversations about a variety of subjects and issues of interest to youngsters.

Bobby's best environment for holding court was the corner drug and soda shop. He had an audience of three to seven open-eyed boys, listening intently to him for hours — a feat that none of our teachers could do in the school classroom. When Bobby was really on a streak, he would order a hamburger, fries, and a milk shake. His followers would order something similar; other people would order Coney Island hot dogs, chips, and sodas. It was difficult for me to understand how and why Bobby could capture our attention when he was not the tallest, fastest, brightest, or best-looking boy among us. Yet, for reasons unknown to me, he was a leader.

Whenever we played football, baseball, or basketball, Bobby was sure to be selected as captain of one of the teams and allowed to choose up sides. He was always allowed to select the position of his choice, but somehow he knew innately how to give his teammates the positions they wanted. We all knew that in football Bobby's position was quarterback; in basketball he would select guard as he was not tall; in baseball it was first base, manager, and/or coach, depending on the circumstances.

I must confess that I envied Bobby's leadership roles simply because I believed that I could do everything better. In certain respects, I realize now that I was not too far off in my assessment. But it was not about my doing things better than Bobby. The key was to have others see me as a leader. For example, Bobby was a struggling C student while I was a handy A student. Yet no one was clamoring around me to discuss current events, news, sports, or the latest movies.

Young nonempowered leaders such as Bobby obtain their leadership status by rising to the occasion at hand. They assume leadership because of an aura that follows them wherever they go. Today we call it charisma or "having presence." Bobby possessed this aura of leadership even when he was not holding court. His presence was evident to everyone when he entered a room.

Coop, meanwhile, was a different kind of leader. To see him was to see what one person called a boy with a "body like Tarzan." Coop's leadership qualities, unlike Bobby's, were based almost exclusively on physical size, abundance of courage, athletic talents, and a commitment to fight anyone who crossed him or a member of his group. He was widely known to protect all members of his group from outside intimidation by school bullies or larger kids. However, he often encouraged physical confrontations among the smaller members of his group.

There were many strange things about Coop's leadership, one of which was that all members of his group were younger, physically smaller, and athletically inferior to him. All members were in awe of him, and totally loyal. I remember the pride I felt when I joined Coop's group. A friend of mine, Louis, and I joined at the same time. We joined primarily because we knew the circus was coming to town and it would be easier to get jobs as a group. Collaboration increased our chances of being employed because together we could assist in setting up the small tents. We also learned that Coop would help us get work if we proved to be all right to him. Ironically, several years later, Louis and I would be hiding from Coop because he threatened to beat up both of us.

To be accepted as a part of Coop's group, we had to undergo a pseudo initiation of demonstrating our loyalty and commitment to his leadership. Coop began our initiation by engaging Louis and me in a marathon-type race consisting of innumerable wind sprints. These wind sprints were designed to let new and old members of the group know, clearly, that Coop would continue to run when everyone else had stopped. Other physical tests of endurance and strength further exemplified his physical superiority.

We learned from other group members that Coop's influence with the circus was based on his size and strength — characteristics needed to set-up large tents — as well as his congenial personality. When we had to compete with larger kids for the few circus positions designated for local kids, all of Coop's group were hired. With Coop around we were unafraid, whether we were going through haunted houses or walking through dark streets and alleys. It was an important time in my life, a period when I had successfully completed all the requirements necessary to join a group. We were family for a short time.

Unfortunately, child leaders, not unlike the adults in the African-American community today, fulfill the supply and demand in a society where large numbers of disenfranchised blacks desire to possess wealth, position, and power outside or inside of society's main institutions. Contrary to many stereotypical beliefs that the majority of African Americans accept mediocrity, the fact is that they seek control of their communities. Even the rising insurgence of gangs reflects a desire to lead and a dream of success and independence.

Today, many young African-American males join gangs and hustle the streets because of a need for recognition, money, and status. These young men's dreams of achieving success within mainstream institutions have been dimmed by racism, insensitivity, and their inability to create a legitimate vision of empowerment. People join gangs primarily to wield power and influence over a community perceived to lack power or influence. These gangs and their leaders seek to give deprived communities leadership while meeting their own demands for recognition and power.

The perception of African-American gangs as a monolithic group of murderers, drug dealers, and criminals is not a valid perception of the gangs' primary objectives. Images of them engaging constantly in criminal activities are used by society to describe the activities of any organization conceived by African Americans to obtain power. The humanitarian efforts of the organizations, no matter what, are nearly always downplayed. For example, during the sixties a number of African American gangs (organizations) were created to empower the black community. Gang leaders such as Stokely Carmichael, H. Rap Brown, Huey Newton, Bobby Seale, and Malcolm X, provided their followers with leadership designed to create success and power for them, either inside or outside the auspices of mainstream institutions.

Officials and law enforcement agents described these leaders and their followers as self-serving communists who posed a dangerous threat to society as well as the African-American community. They failed to see the positive effects these leaders had in redistributing power to create successes for people cornered within inner-city ghettoes.

African-American leaders, whether in a gang or a political organization, have a tremendous amount of influence and control over their followers. Until the 1990s, they provided leadership from nonempowered positions, seeking only to extract concessions from the institutions or to create a separate but equal power base within the society. However, during the past two decades and continuing to the present, we have become familiar with various African-American leaders who lobby the European-American-owned companies to persuade them to do business with minority-owned businesses.

According to the researchers, of the billions of dollars spent each year by the European-American-owned companies, less than 5 percent was spent with minority contractors. The statistics did not show, but we all know, that more than 95 percent of the purchases made by African Americans went to European-American-owned businesses. These spending practices play a major role in perpetuating the successes that these businesses enjoy.

Researchers also did not mention that if African Americans had bought billions of dollars of goods and services from African-American-owned businesses, there would not be a need to constantly lobby European Americans to "do the right thing." But as we all know our philosophical thrust has been to seek concessions (limited power) from the European-American companies by asking them to do a small portion of their business with African Americans. We believed that if we could open the door and become the first to get a contract, then other blacks will follow and, because of our efforts, both whites and blacks will perceive us as leaders.

Unfortunately, some African-American leaders support the philosophy of former President Ronald Reagan, suggesting that the great wealth of a few businesses will trickle down to improve the conditions of the masses. The trickle down theory has been promoted for years by various philosophers and economists who fervently argue that if the rich get richer, the poor will get a share, no matter how small.

Today, many African-American leaders have modified the trickle down theory to mean that if African Americans work, eat, and sleep with European Americans, they are better off than those who are unable to do so. They believe that no matter how bad the overall conditions might be for blacks as a whole, those who obtain positions with European Americans improve the chances for success for others.

The masses of African Americans were taught to follow black leaders who advocated teaching children to talk, walk, look, and act as much like European Americans as possible. This was supposed to enhance their opportunities to obtain a good job or a business contract with a European-American business. What this means is African Americans were taught that success in contemporary America hinged on meeting certain standards established by European Americans. It is no small wonder that when African Americans were given the choice to support their own institutions, including businesses, schools, and clubs, they elected to seek integration and support European-American institutions at the expense of our "separate, but equal" institutions.

The point being made here is not an argument for or against integration, but an illustration of how a lack of economic and cultural resources prevented blacks from successfully integrating with another ethnic group who, by definition, viewed them as inferior beings. Instead of strengthening their institutions, blacks abandoned them and, in the process, gave up a limited version of empowerment.

I do not believe for a moment that an economic system that displaces millions of workers and condones open begging on city streets, blatant discrimination, widespread violence, proliferation of jails, and market manipulation should be viewed as a panacea for African Americans. There is no doubt in my mind that we can create and manage businesses capable of successfully competing with, at a minimum, Frito Lay, Pepsi, Coca Cola, Nike, Reebok, Safeway, Lucky's, Macy's, Hilton, Hyatt, and many others.

Today, can blacks expect from European Americans anything better than what they can do for themselves? Do blacks believe European Americans will share their power and wealth faster and more efficiently than blacks can create and develop their own empowerment structure? If African Americans are to achieve self-empowerment, future leaders (empowerment surrogates) must come from an empowered group. They must be practitioners of the principles of empowerment, which includes the people they desire to inspire and remind of their inherent power. Their leadership must be free of fear, worry, envy, and daily struggle.

During the nineties, the decade of empowerment, African-American leaders will share their visions of how to remove the chains of ignorance that bind blacks together as victims. They will share the limitless powers of their vision with people who have lived centuries just trying to survive.

Suggestions for Creating Empowered Beliefs of Leadership

1. Describe your definition of a leader.

2. When did you first become aware of the need for leadership?

3. Do you perceive yourself as a leader?

4. Describe at least five qualities a leader must possess.

5. How many of these qualities do you possess?

6. Reconnect with your vision of empowerment and envision your self as a faceless, colorless, and formless being.

7. As a faceless, colorless, and formless being, are you aware of the need for leadership?

8. Describe five qualities that are essential for one to express empowered leadership.

9. Do you presently possess any of these qualities?

10. Who led you to your intuitive self?

CHAPTER TEN
SUCCESS AND FAILURE

I am empowered whenever I can say, "I see the success in you that I see in myself."

When one is a six-year-old first grader, success and failure can cause you to believe that every success is good and every failure is bad. Unfortunately, I was preoccupied with perfection (success) and terrified of imperfection (failure) simply because Guides were teaching me to embrace success and shun failure. They did not teach me how to cope with setbacks (failures) experienced by all of us at some time in our lives.

Unfortunately, some African Americans, like me, confronted failure at a very early age. For example, I was terrified of not achieving perfection in the first grade. Perfection in learning was my cardinal rule. It was considered imperfect learning to have a first grade student stand before his classmates to recite the alphabet and say, "*a, b, c, d, f, h, i, j, l,* " and not understand that the correct sequence had been broken.

When a six year old is translating his best efforts into failures, such results will undoubtedly affect how he views success. It becomes easy to understand how young children grow into adults who are terrified of failing. As small children, we were rewarded when we got the correct answer to the problem. We received this reward whether we worked with or without a teacher.

A six year old victim cannot ever imagine success within a larger community context. Accomplishments for a six year old are not considered accomplishments for a sixteen year old, a twenty one year old or a thirty year old. Success, by definition, is connected causally to failure. The distinguishing factor is whether the accomplishment is seen as greater than the accomplishments of someone else. Sometimes even an accomplishment is perceived as failure. For example, inventing the automobile, airplane, Xerox copier, or television before society is ready may be perceived as a failure rather than a success. Timing is important.

Unfortunately, most victims envision success as their only reason for living; failure is seen as the pain and humiliation one must pass through to reach success. Most often we prefer to have success without passing through failures. However, the road to empowerment is paved with both failures and successes, so that the traveler becomes engulfed with pain and joy. He or she remains in the state of emotional agitation until able to work through these powerful states. Then the traveler is using the powers of intuitive knowing.

Like anything else in life that we strive to achieve, success is relative. Most stories from successful people are filled with accounts of overcoming many obstacles. The first step is to decide what you really want to do and then, like the child learning to walk, persevere until you reach your goal. However, we all know this is easier said than done.

No first step is accomplished without exerting some effort. Child psychologists argue that a young child's desire to walk overcomes his fear of falling. No matter how many times the child falls, he or she invariably will, unless hampered by physical or psychological problems, persevere. The child who learns to walk must also learn to talk, read, count, and solve a countless number of emotional and practical problems during life on earth. It is the child's potential to solve problems and overcome obstacles that decides how well he or she will succeed in life.

Throughout most of our lives we try to escape from one of the most powerful obstacles that governs the nonempowered mind, namely, failure. Failure, or the fear of challenging failure, is something that prevents many victims from moving from point a, (the idea) to point b, (the effect).

When you decide what you really want to do in life, you face a mountain of information on why it cannot be done. Doubt forms as you receive all the data on how your idea will not work or that what you are talking about has already been tried.

When an unsuccessful person hears this information from family, friends, or persons whom he holds in high esteem, it is normally enough to stop the action needed to implement the idea. Why? Is an unsuccessful person physically and mentally inferior to a successful person? Have you ever stopped to wonder why some people achieve success in a given area while others who seek success in the same area fail? Is it attributed to luck? Is it the blessing of God? Is it plain hard work, or is it a belief in one's ability to achieve goals?

Most of the successful people whom we read about in books tend to have a serious aura around their persona. They do not let a day pass by without thinking about and working toward their desired goals. They are able to overcome or control the worldly distractions of self-aggrandizement by adhering to a program of discipline when carefully-made plans do not work.

I recently heard a great basketball player talk about how much he loved basketball and how much time he devoted to practicing techniques to improve his game. Apparently, from his television account, his love of basketball was a greater priority to him than his desire for a wife at this particular point in his life. He believed that if he married, he would not be able to devote the requisite time to a family and still play basketball at the level he desired to play. He believed that a wife would require that he make their successful marriage his main priority. He was unprepared to bring into his life a person who might not have the same high level of interest and commitment to basketball. I imagined similar answers coming from Florence Joyner (track star), Whitney Houston (entertainer), or Dr. Alvin Poussiant (Harvard professor), and Dr. Johnetta Cole (Spelman College president).

We are all born with the basic equal desires to walk, talk, and overcome the routine obstacles of childhood. It is generally agreed that children achieve these goals at about the same time in life. According to the "data gatherers," there does not appear to be any data to suggest that a child who is slow to walk or talk is less or more successful than one who learns faster. However, we already know from our life experiences that at some point a dichotomy between successful and unsuccessful characteristics begins to develop among equal children.

Many knowledgeable people theorize that the success/failure dichotomy begins as early as a child's first encounter with school. Supposedly during this time successful children begin to discipline themselves, define academic and personal goals, and accept responsibility for their actions.

We are familiar with stories of incorrigible children who become successful adults. No doubt they possessed an intense desire and a belief in themselves to achieve predetermined goals in spite of society's characterization of them. They were serious about what they wanted to do. By contrast, the majority of African-American adults who began their life's journey socially unequal are judged by the world as being unsuccessful. Their success is not determined by accomplishments, but is defined by race. As judged by American society and perhaps the global world society, African Americans are perceived as a population of failures.

When I was a boy, I knew many successful African Americans, although society may not have viewed them as such. I did not think maids, janitors, cooks, dishwashers, and laborers were failures. When

I saw them walking their children to school, I saw pride in their steps and faces. When I saw them feed hungry kids, like me, I felt their love and compassion for blackness. When I heard them speak in a language barely discernible as English, I saw the pain or humiliation in their eyes. And when I used the same words, they said, "Boy, you ain't going to school to learn to talk like that. On Sundays, when I observed them seated in church to hear a good "message" and receive "salvation from the Lord," I felt a sense of belonging to a powerful community. Undoubtedly my views of the world were limited at the time. But those wonderful African-American people were not failures or inferior to anyone.

Since then, when I have been faced with seemingly impossible problems, there have been many days when memories of successful African Americans returned to rescue me from my doubts. When my thoughts were preoccupied with doubts and failures, I reminded myself of the millions of African Americans who experienced equally difficult problems, and yet were able to reach out to give love, compassion, food, clothes, shelter, and encouragement to others.

Whenever I recall these experiences, my child consciousness does not allow doubts and failures to prevent me from moving forward with actions to reach my desired goals. However, my adult consciousness allows me to think and consider problems that may cause me not to succeed. In this state of awareness, I fail to realize that all my experiences provide the power I need to overcome any obstacle.

On the road to empowerment, we use our vision of inner power to assist others in remembering a time when they were free from concerns of failure. We use this vision to stimulate the mind to use its intuitive powers. Unfortunately, many of us allow our actions to be interpreted and judged by others. Even when we believe we are successful, we wait for someone to validate us. Once we accept their opinions as the criteria, we then judge our successes based on material gain: houses, cars, clothes, and so on. This causes us to visualize success and failure within the limited context of nonempowered thinking.

Many European Americans define success in the business world as acquiring a position of leadership in a Fortune 500 company. The nonempowered African American defines success in the same way, hoping additionally that attitudes about African Americans will change so that future generations can also become company leaders.

The European-American institutions can take any nonempowered African American, regardless of his or her relative position and status in the African-American community, and transform that person into a success by allowing him to join their institutions. Even if in a nonrevenue-generating corporate position, such as a personnel manager for a Fortune 500 company, he or she is viewed as more successful than a person who works as a CEO for an African-American-owned business.

The European American definition of success requires that society maintain a standard whereby all achievements in education, moral principles, ethics, law, religion, medicine, and so on are defined by European Americans. To change this criterion and acknowledge African Americans for their accomplishments in these areas would destroy the European American definition of success. In other words, if African Americans controlled the stock ownership and corporate leadership of at least one hundred of the Fortune 500 companies, then society's definitions of success and failure would change.

I am convinced that the failure rate for the masses of African Americans increases significantly when visions for success become rooted in definitions established by a society which views blacks as failures.

According to some sociologists, African Americans live in America primarily to receive recognition from society that some of their deeds are successful. That is, their goal is to receive a rating of success from society. For many African Americans, not to receive a success rating renders all their accomplishments as failures. For those African Americans who use the principles of empowerment, success continues to be an outpouring of limitlessness.

To perceive successes for what they are, we must first reject society's criteria for evaluating success and failure. We then become guided by the success empowerment dictum: "I see the success in you that I see in myself."

Suggestions for Creating New Beliefs of Success and Failure

1. When did you first discern the difference between success and failure?

2. Did you feel a sense of joy and pride during those moments you perceived yourself as a success?

3. Did you feel a sense of sadness and rejection during those moments you perceived yourself as a failure?

4. What steps did you take to overcome beliefs of failure?

5. Reconnect with your vision of empowerment and envision yourself as a faceless, colorless, and formless being.

6. As a faceless, colorless, and formless being, do you perceive yourself existing within the scope of success and failure?

7. Describe your perception of success from an empowered awareness.

8. Describe your perception of failure from an empowered awareness.

9. In this state of awareness, do you have the power to redefine your actions?

CHAPTER ELEVEN
RACISM

Racism is a misguided belief of power and superiority over another person.

I live in a country where nearly everyone admits that racism exists, but very few people will admit being racist. For example, among the 535 members of congress, there are no confessed racists. No one among the members of the president's cabinet is racist. All the presidents of the Fortune 1000 companies, public education universities, television and radio stations, newspaper publishers and major religious denominations are not racists. We can continue this list to include state governors, city mayors, police chiefs, and nearly every position with authority and not find a self-proclaimed racist among them. Where, then, are all the racists that we know exist in this country?

Racism is not a small matter for African Americans traveling on the road to empowerment. It can prevent a willing neophyte from becoming empowered because of its perceived effects. Racism makes victims of African-American children at an early age. As an African-American male, I experienced racial discrimination and hatred quite early in life. Since I spent some of my childhood living in Texas, I can tell horror stories of being called demeaning names and of witnessing similar treatment of others.

Unfortunately, at every juncture in my life I have been affected by the white supremacist philosophy. It suggests that the white race is superior to all others and therefore should be in charge of the institutions that control our lives. Almost all the information that I received from public school teachers, parents, and other adults reinforced the philosophy of white superiority and the inferior, unequal status for blacks.

I experience the pain all over whenever I recall being taught to believe that, because of my color, I was not represented by the doctrine which declares "all men are created equal." It was demeaning and punitive to know that society's professed "democracy for all" excluded me and millions of others like me from the opportunities to grow and develop into the people that we envision ourselves becoming. As far back as I remember, other African Americans tried to counteract this by motivating me to study hard so I could grow up to be "somebody." However, this need to be "somebody" implanted in me the idea that I was nobody.

As a young strong African-American boy full of youth, vigor, and determination, I believed I was capable of accomplishing whatever I wanted. For some innate reason, I just didn't see myself as being unequal to whites or anyone else during my youth.

I can recall my dreams as a young boy of becoming a top athlete. Athletes represented overt success within both the European and African American societies, even though the degree of success between them was measurably different. I dreamed of becoming a Jackie Robinson, Roy Capenella, Don Newcombe, Joe Louis, or Sugar Ray Robinson. I, and thousands of other youngsters, gave very little thought to the hundreds of other baseball players and boxers who toiled away at their professions, but were unable to reach stardom. I think when given the choice, we always choose to be on top.

Growing up as an African-American youth in a race consciousness society, I learned to believe that my dreams of success would be conditioned by the color of my skin. I was taught that although I may have dreams of being "number one" in a given profession, it was impossible for me to achieve that status and recognition from society because of my race.

Baseball player Hank Aaron hit more career home runs than the previous record holder, Babe Ruth. Ricky Henderson stole more career bases than Ty Cobb. But in both of these cases, I doubt that the record breakers can ever lay claim to truly being number one in the hearts and minds of the majority of Americans. European-American children will not daydream about becoming like Hank Aaron.

Society's obsession with being number one requires all of us to think in terms of being superior to all others whom we pass on our way to the top. Conversely, those individuals whom we pass are taught to think of themselves as being inferior. Once they accept this belief, they seek to establish power over individuals on the social ladder beneath them.

This feeling of superiority is introduced to us in subtle and innocuous messages. In my case, it began with my eagerness to learn and trust new things about the world. At this stage, I was not aware of racism nor did I understand its effects on the people in my life. My lack of understanding and awareness did not mean that racism was not present. Only that society used education and teaching resources to introduce racism to eager unsuspecting minds. The subject was introduced as gradually and effortlessly as the abc's and the English language.

Learning the alphabet was no small matter, particularly in my case, because of the warnings I received from second-and third-grade friends about how difficult it was. They told me that the most difficult part of school was learning the abc's, how to print your name, spell correctly, stand and read from the Dick, Jane, and Spot textbook, and sit in your seat while the teacher talked. I had serious doubts about my ability to do these things successfully. My lack of self-confidence was totally unrelated to race or intelligence. I simply didn't think I could sit quietly in a seat long enough to learn to read, write, and count.

Contrary to the information I received from my friends, the first grade turned out to be the first place I ever achieved anything outside my family circle. For the first time in my life, I was conscious of feeling very good about myself and my abilities to learn something new. My accomplishments gave me confidence, as I learned the alphabet in record speed, spelled all the required words, and could print my name and read before the class. In fact, it was in the first grade that I began to use education to overcompensate for my lack of material possessions.

I'll never forget the day when my first grade teacher told me that I was smart. I was so proud to know that I was not dumb that I ran the few short blocks to my house to tell mother about how smart I was. Like most of African-American mothers of my youth, my mother appeared to be physically tired all the time. She apparently was able to cope with hard work, racism, a demanding son, and still maintain her mental composure. I realize now that she was far more patient in coping with society's racism and with me than I am, sometimes, with my son.

My mother encouraged me to keep studying hard, and with every chance she got she told her friends how smart her boy was. In her own way, I suppose she must have found great joy in knowing that I was not dumb. To be perceived by adults as being dumb did not mean that a child was incapable of learning, but that he would be relegated to a life of menial work as a janitor, laborer, waiter, dishwasher, fry cook, or some other position reserved for poorly educated African Americans.

To be labeled "smart" meant you had the potential to become a school teacher, doctor, dentist, insurance salesman, federal government worker, or any other profession available to African Americans who were considered relatively literate. Since I was smart, I wanted to become another George Washington Carver, Booker T. Washington, or Ralph Bunche. I understood that first I had to learn the correct spelling of all the words listed in the index of the first grade reader. Then my teacher could promote me to the second grade. Some of those words (animal, clothes, together, circus, tricycle) were challenges for me.

So I adjusted to the demands of school and in doing so I accepted a learning process designed to teach me that I was unequal to European Americans. I was validating the power of my educators to teach me "the truth" about myself. Once I accepted this line of reasoning, I was on the road to accepting my role as a victim of racism. Later in life, after carrying my wounds from racism for a long time, I resented the teachers and other adults who were accomplices in an educational system that teaches African-American children how to function as victims in a racist society.

Racism was my constant companion throughout my secondary and postsecondary education. It engulfed me so subtly and completely that I was unaware I was its victim. Once I became an adult, I couldn't discern the reasons why I disliked other African Americans and myself. The powers of racism were so great that I wanted to become something other than what I was.

Racism had engulfed me and all those around me without ever letting us know we were its victims. My mother was its victim. She was a maid just like millions of other African-American women of her time. Although she didn't finish high school or attend college, she had good common sense. My mother and I lived in a society where African Americans' desires constantly fluctuated between ambition and acquiescence. She did not dwell on the outside effects of racism as much as I would as an adult. She seemed to have accepted her position in the world and appeared to be seeking a modicum of dignity while living the inferior life designed for her by society.

Nonetheless, I know that my mother desired to see me become more than she perceived herself to be. It was no different among my friends Bobby, Charles, and Louis. All of our parents wanted us to become empowered enough to make things better for millions of other African Americans. They accepted racial abuse to provide us with the opportunity to become empowered adults who, unlike them, would be free.

Society tried to teach our parents, like the slave parents before them, to believe they were racially inferior. They probably, however, didn't accept these views of themselves unconditionally. They lived in an era when racism was clearly accepted by society. During this period, European Americans did not publicly deny their racist views of African Americans. It was considered unthinkable for African Americans to claim they were empowered and free of racism.

Three decades later, I can freely say that I have appropriated empowered consciousness to reject society's teachings of racism. I can and do use the principles of empowerment to make decisions about people, things, and life. Many of you may question how I can firmly and unequivocally state that I use empowered consciousness in a country that, as a whole, is perceived to be more racist now than ever before? How do I know that I am no longer its prisoner?

Whenever you tap into intuitive consciousness, you automatically access images that are free of rational beliefs. Whenever you use this power, racism loses its power over you. Intuitive knowing allows you to achieve empowerment regardless of where you live. I lay claim to my freedom from racism simply by knowing it has no power over my abilities to express my vision of empowerment. I am no longer a prisoner because I released the chains of skin color from my body and the victim-consciousness acid from my mind. When I appropriated intuitive consciousness as the way to freedom, I healed my wounds from racism and forgave myself for believing in something as ludicrous as being unequal to someone else. (I also forgave myself for spending so much time seeking success in people and things outside of myself.)

I can positively say that when you use the powers of intuitive consciousness you are no longer able to accept a racist philosophy. Even those African Americans who served as society's slaves, segregated workers, and integrated European clones had the powers of intuitive consciousness available for their use. However, intuitive consciousness was not the option chosen by those blacks who lived as victims under the kingdom of racism.

Whenever victims rely exclusively on rational consciousness for their freedom, they are doomed to live hoping that freedom will come. They live for a future which doesn't include them. They live as victims with hope that the future world will be a better place for their children. Empowerment always exists in the present. To look to the future for answers is to deny your power to fully express yourself now in the midst of racism.

My mother and most of her peers have now died. They escaped racism by physically leaving its clutches. As their offspring, it is our responsibility to empower ourselves to be free physically and mentally while we live in a racist world every day. Unfortunately, to do this, we must transcend the damage done to us and our parents by rebuilding our family structure from a base of empowerment. We cannot forget racism's role in destroying the black family structure. It did not allow black men to recognize themselves as men, or to perceive their sons becoming something other than themselves. That's the way it was with my father. He had no influence on my childhood development and his absence deprived me of a father figure during the early stages of my life. However, I vicariously adopted other men as father figures to help me set goals and work toward becoming a man.

While I encourage all African-American males to accept responsibility for educating their children, I don't ask the children to become defeated victims when the father is absent. A person born with black skin sometimes finds that the conditions and circumstances of life do not afford the opportunity to have both parents living together during his or her childhood. But if both parents are not actively participating in your development, it really doesn't matter. I do not believe an African-American child living with both parents will be free of racism any more so than a child with one or no parents. It's even possible that it may be worse for some children who lose respect for their fathers because their fathers don't measure up to society's definition of men.

No, I do not believe African American children are more victimized by racism because of the absence of their fathers. But the effects of being taught to hate ourselves over several generations has allowed racism to make us its prisoners. Racism robbed our minds and stripped our bodies to make us ashamed of ourselves. In spite of its damage to us and our knowledge of its cause, many African Americans still seek out others to define its meaning.

Ideally, it is better for both parents to be living together. But there are millions of African-American children living in single-parent homes. It would be self-defeating to tell them they cannot accomplish their visions for success simply because their parents are separated. This is analogous to telling people they cannot achieve their vision of empowerment because of skin color. The important thing is for the caregiver to instill love and confidence in the child so that he or she can envision empowerment regardless of living conditions.

Empowerment teaches African-American children not to perceive themselves as inferior simply because society has decreed them to be so because they do not meet the family or racial criteria for being average. I feel good when I tell someone that I'm free from the powers of racism. Every day that it seeks to re-incarcerate me, I claim my inherent empowered consciousness. In this state of awareness I understand that racism is a belief embodied by powerless people who need something to distinguish themselves from other people with different skin colors.

Suggestions for Transcending Beliefs of Racism

1. Describe your first experience with racism.

2. Did your first experience with racism cause you to become angry and bitter toward the person(s) involved?

3. Describe three beliefs that you embodied from this experience.

4. Describe three beliefs that you transcended from this experience.

5. What was your role in your first experience with racism: victim or oppressor?

6. Describe the reasons why you interpreted your role in this manner?

7. Reconnect with your vision of empowerment and envision yourself as a faceless, colorless, and formless being.

8. As a faceless, colorless, and formless being, are you aware of racism?

9. Describe racism from your awareness as a faceless, colorless, and formless being. Are you a victim or oppressor?

10. Describe yourself outside the context of racism.

CHAPTER TWELVE
EQUALITY

I am equal the moment I accept myself as an equal part of creation.

When I was a six-year-old boy, freedom meant having unlimited time to play with my friends, along with having all the material things that I believed represented success. I was living in such wretched conditions that my thoughts of food, clothing, and housing prevented me from thinking about empowerment. Like so many African-American children of the fifties and sixties, I grew up focusing on individual pleasures and folklore about the "good old days."

I was aware that white people "had everything" while my limited material possessions reflected my status as a victim. Society had taught me to stay in my place — a place that was obviously inferior to that of whites. Both races generally accepted such ideas to the degree that we thought we had no possible chance of obtaining the quality of life offered to most whites. It did not matter how much education we had. Some African Americans had more education than a significant number of European Americans. Yet they did not have power or influence over even poor and illiterate whites.

Contrary to some popular European-American beliefs, my childhood thoughts were not about being equal to whites, but about how to obtain the essential things in life. I desired to become a man formed in the images of other black men. I did not see myself as a boy who would grow up to become a cloned white man. My definition of black manhood emerged out of my observations of the black men around me. Even as a young boy, I saw freedom and empowerment present in black manhood. If I listened to others and used my senses as a guide, I would become the man that I wanted to be.

I now realize that all the information I received from my mother, teachers, relatives, and elders was well-intentioned, but rooted in a world of misinformation and deprivation. [*different era*] When my parents, teachers and leaders of society told me I could be anything I wanted to be, I seriously doubt they really believed what they said. I suspect they were trying to inspire me to think, study, and grow up to be successful in a position befitting a black male. [?]

I grew up in a society governed by hypocrisy. Because this society was psychologically unprepared to accept a population of empowered African Americans, none of the existing institutions desired to educate and empower them. But empowerment is not about judging existing institutions and past injustices. It begins by relinquishing our aspirations to be equal to European Americans and accepting the evidence of our innate greatness.

Unfortunately, today we are continuing our efforts to define appropriate roles for African Americans in a society preoccupied with marketing the values and symbols of white superiority. In spite of this intense marketing campaign, which depicts the majority of African Americans as victims, I still do not understand why the masses of African Americans do not control neighborhoods that other ethnic groups, including our own, find appealing. Is there an inherent [?] abnormality associated with African-American lifestyles that people, including blacks, find so unpleasant that they would not be able to enjoy a meal, or a stroll, or would not shop in the chic boutiques located in a black-owned and controlled neighborhood?

Is the African American's personality so entrenched with negative images that a success-oriented marketing campaign is rendered unbelievable? Is the perception of blackness so rooted in failure that the African American is incapable of visualizing, naturally, blackness as representing success? It is inconceivable, if one is honest with one's self, to think of a predominately white neighborhood in San Francisco, Washington, D.C., Houston, or Los Angeles as being an area where other ethnic groups would not desire to live. On the other hand, it's just as inconceivable to think of a predominately black neighborhood in the same cities as being a desirable area where other ethnic groups would desire to live. Why?

Well, it seems to me that there are three main differences between the two neighborhoods: (1) the neighborhood hierarchical status; (2) the aesthetic qualities of the buildings, people, and the social community; and (3) requisite businesses to support the residents of the communities, such as banks, quality supermarkets, clothing stores, and quality restaurants. If we accept these reasons as sufficient, at least as a basis for discussion, then we can begin to work toward changing the African-American neighborhoods to reflect not so much the desires of other ethnic groups, but the desires of African Americans.

Some prominent black leaders constantly remind us that we spend billions of dollars each year on goods produced outside black neighborhoods. Yet as of today African Americans still do not manufacture or distribute many basic consumer goods.

Nevertheless, let's assume that African Americans spend their money outside the black community because of an inherent socio-economic ethos, which perceives black businesses as being inferior to the mainstream definitions of success. In Oakland, California, where I have lived most of my life, African Americans represent the largest ethnic group, yet one of the smallest ethnic groups — Asian Americans — owns and operates more diverse businesses on a per capita basis.

The Asian-American community has been able to carve out a part of the city and attract other ethnic groups, including African Americans, on a regular basis. The key is not so much that other ethnic groups patronize the Asian businesses, but that their base of support is the Asian-American community. Obviously, Asian Americans are able to produce successful businesses because of their cultural values that support their own communities. African Americans, however, believe that whatever they own is not as good as what European Americans own.

African Americans cannot continue to educate our young people in old ideas rooted in a stagnant philosophy of inferiority. Today is the decade of freedom of choice. We must choose to invest our lives and communities with images of success. We need to join in creating businesses to fill the needs of our communities as well as those of other communities. We must establish new agendas and shape new priorities.

We cannot be so preoccupied with criticizing every ethnic group while our own failures are exempt from any criticism. In fact, our unwritten policy of not publicly criticizing other African Americans, in spite of their ineffectiveness, has cost us very dearly. African Americans cannot afford to discuss our dislikes privately amongst ourselves and then have our inaction translated into apathy.

Furthermore, we cannot let our long-held beliefs and feelings prevent us from empowering our thoughts and actions. Each day traveled on the road to empowerment is filled with many opportunities to fall back into previously discarded habits and ideas. Some days are filled with an abundance of joy while many others are occupied by constant depression.

Certainly the vicissitudes of joy and depression exist on the road to empowerment. On a given day, our lives are affected by a steady dosage of negative perceptions of African Americans as intellectually and biologically deficient, and therefore not quite equal to European Americans. For example, a recent local newspaper article reveals that when seeking employment, black males were not treated the same as white males. The study found, among many other problems, that employers still preferred white males over black males. Ironically, the reporter interjects a certain disbelief that the study confirmed what most people already knew: blacks do not receive equal privileges and treatment afforded to whites. This disbelief is what drives society to make minor alterations to its policies to accommodate the needs of African Americans. It is a half-hearted attempt to address the causes of inequitable treatment of blacks.

Meanwhile, someone in the government has devised a method of changing standardized tests to give African Americans additional points to raise their scores to equal European Americans' test level. That is, if an African American's test score was 50 and a European American's test score was 80, then the African American's score would be raised to 80 to compensate for cultural inequities. This is a strange way to achieve equality.

African Americans should not be totally dependent upon European Americans for jobs. Dependency, by definition, gives authority and control to someone else to make decisions regarding your life. Dependency, coupled with all the gloom and doom about African-American males, could cause you to become depressed and give up the fight for empowerment. But we all know that the news media only reveal what African Americans have known for many decades: society perceives blacks to be an inferior race of people. The question that follows is, What can be done about it?

First, African-American entrepreneurs should make an effort to recruit, hire, and train young black men to work in their businesses.

Second, unemployed African-American males with the education, skills, and work experience should market themselves to companies that have a global perspective on hiring employees.

Third, African-American college graduates should use their education to create jobs and opportunities for themselves and the masses of unemployed African Americans.

Fourth, African-American teachers and parents should include in their goals an agenda that exposes young people to alternatives for achieving success. Our youth should know that employment with a large European-American company is not the only measure of achievement.

Fifth, African Americans must shed their perceptions of themselves as victims and take bold steps to act as a group with a defined purpose. Changes cannot occur unless people perceive and implement the action necessary for changes

During the past thirty years or so, since the "War on Poverty," African Americans have accepted the notion that they were deficient in education, skills, culture, and experiences when compared to other groups of people. (There is, however, a big difference in not having opportunities to be educated and obtain job experience, and having those opportunities and not using them.)

African Americans, in a short span of three decades, have accomplished many great feats in spite of various inequalities. If we accomplished great feats in medicine, religion, education and business without a collective agenda, just imagine how much higher we can soar with more knowledge and a planned agenda of empowerment. The manipulations of test scores, the continuous racial discrimination in the hiring of African Americans, the perils of drugs, crime, and poverty are not enough to thwart our success in empowering ourselves to accomplish even greater things.

The African-American community must resist the expediency of trying to defend itself to a community that knows little or nothing about what blacks "really want." The steps taken to uplift blacks, whether affirmative action, quotas, or job training programs, are rooted in a belief system that blacks are an inferior race of people in need of help before they can assimilate, as a group, into the dominant society. African Americans must abandon such beliefs and envision themselves as equal to all humans. Once this consciousness is achieved, then our work will not be about uplifting the race to become equal to whites, but to achieve empowerment.

African Americans have the resources to accomplish any goals, overcome any obstacles, and achieve great levels of success. We can collectively (1) invest our monies and resources in an infrastructure controlled by African Americans; (2) train children to seek alternatives to eliminate lack and limitation; and (3) prepare an agenda and action plan to build a prosperous community.

One of the first steps African Americans should take is to change their views of themselves as inferior and to see through eyes of empowerment. The empowered mind always selects the successful outcome over the unsuccessful. Many African Americans living in cities throughout the United States are on the verge of becoming extremely successful without even realizing it. It may seem strange to the nonempowered thinking mind, which only believes that our communities are about to be destroyed by drugs, crime, unemployment, lack of adequate businesses, and so on. However, empowered minds do not consider it strange to see order and success in the midst of chaos and failure.

African Americans are finally in the position to break away from the parent/child relationship we have had to endure since we began our sojourn in this country as slaves. We can now tap into the powers of intuitive consciousness and create a vision of empowerment. We can use the principles of empowerment to remove the appearances of failure all around us. The fact that crime, drugs and unemployment are omnipresent in most African Americans' lives is nothing more than an illusion which show us what we do not want to embrace.

The vision of empowerment clearly reveals that we do not want to create an economic and social philosophy based on class or gender that discriminates against those who do not meet its criteria for membership. We do not want an economic system that has adult males hanging out in parking lots or standing on street corners during normal business hours. We do not want to see people who use drugs and alcohol to compensate for the continued feeling of powerlessness. We also do not want to see people who resort to murder, robbery, and theft against other African Americans in vain attempts to acquire "respect" or manhood. Nor do we want to see people who, based on the illusion of permanent victimhood, have become so turned off with their lives that they have given up and lost their natural creativity and power.

(Moreover, we do not want African-American women to believe that it is their role and responsibility to be the head of the household) or that it is a natural way of life for a poor African-American family not to have a male in a contributing role. We do not want African-American women to perceive themselves as competing with African-American men and fighting over status and recognition from society.

We do want to work from a position of empowerment to develop a work ethic that is rooted in positiveness and creativity. We want to ensure that our children have opportunities to work and accomplish their dreams of success.

We can use our intuitive knowing to develop a community where individuals with group empowered consciousness fully understand their relationship to each other.

We can have African-American college graduates use their engineering, architectural, and planning degrees to design and construct bridges, dams, and commercial buildings. We can have our college graduates put their marketing, insurance, accounting, business, and other degrees to work for African-American businesses or become business owners themselves.

We can discipline black high school graduates to obtain job training by working for African-American-owned businesses, where they will acquire an understanding of a new philosophy of black business.

An empowered African-American community will not try to solve all of its problems at once. Sufficient time and energy must be devoted to creating new opportunities for growth. Yes, we are all concerned about the unpleasant things around us and would like for someone to remove them for us. Unfortunately, the responsibility starts with those who have the vision and who see great opportunities in our present situation, rather than depression and despair.

During a recent discussion, a colleague reminded me that African Americans are always developing an "agenda." However, before we can get six months into the implementation phase, we become so engulfed with daily personal survival needs that we forget what the original agenda was. We forget that our original agenda was to uplift a race of people. It's like being in a lake up to your neck fighting alligators. It is difficult to remember that your original reason for being in the water was to dredge the lake.

Similarly, when African Americans accept their individual lives as powerless, it becomes difficult for individuals to join with others in perceiving the collective African-American community as powerful.

Our perception of ourselves should originate from an empowered mind. The empowered African-American mind does not make decisions from the victim consciousness of lack and limitation, but from the consciousness of ownership, power, and abundance. Once we understand the use of intuitive knowing, it renders our previous fight for equality a finished battle.

Suggestions for Transcending Beliefs of Equality

1. At what age did you first become aware that some people were considered unequal to others?

2. What was your perception of yourself during this experience: equal or unequal?

3. Describe three qualities that a person must have to be considered part of the equal class.

4. How many of these qualities do you possess?

5. If you lack the qualities that place you in the equal class of society, then do you desire to possess these qualities?

6. Reconnect with your vision of empowerment and envision your self as a faceless, colorless, and formless being. Are you aware of the need for beliefs of equality?

7. Describe equality from your awareness as a faceless, colorless, and formless being.

8. As a faceless, colorless, and formless being, do you lack equality within the scope of your purpose?

CHAPTER THIRTEEN
EDUCATION

Education is a system created from the belief that someone knows something worth sharing. Those who have education are believed to be better off than those without it.

When I was a little boy, my mother told me that the "only way a colored man can get ahead in this country is to get a good education." At the time, during the fifties, African Americans considered education a higher priority than registering to vote would be during the sixties. To the masses of uneducated blacks, education represented a form of freedom.

Most victims consider education to be the foundation for all learning and development. All that we are reflects our education. Reading this book requires a certain level of education, just as writing it required a certain level of education. Humans created education to organize their descriptions of their physical and emotional environment.

One can easily argue that prior to education, someone felt the need to create words to name things, such as rivers, mountains, trees, flowers, grass, sun, moon, etc. One can also imagine that the early purpose of education was to enhance communication and perpetuate knowledge. It is highly unlikely that the first use of education was to prepare someone for a job or career.

Moreover, one can safely argue that the current curriculum used by teachers at all levels fosters the notion that the greater the knowledge the students have of English, mathematics, history, and practical concepts, the greater the level of success they can expect to achieve in society. Education is an important tool for the empowerment of African Americans; however, we must understand its limitations.

As a tool for African-American empowerment, education was key to the philosophies of leaders such as Booker T. Washington,

W.E.B. Du Bois, and Martin Luther King, Jr. A quality education represented the opportunity for African Americans to obtain jobs and receive decent salaries to buy the necessary primary goods that enhanced their status in the society, that is, education allowed African Americans the opportunity to work in less ostensibly slave-oriented positions.

In contemporary society, the goals of education are to prepare African Americans to obtain jobs in businesses. Many have used education to try to change the prevailing views of themselves as nonempowered people. Consequently, generations of well-educated African Americans, working for European Americans, have helped create profitable businesses such as Wells Fargo Bank, Frito Lay, Sears, Chevron, Shell, Macy's, R.J. Reynolds, Kellogg's, newspaper dailies in every major city, Nike, Coca Cola, Burger King, Kentucky Fried Chicken, Coors, Seagrams, and numerous other companies. The list could go on to include all the products and services mass- produced, distributed, and sold in this country.

Ironically, the stock ownership of all these companies is controlled exclusively by non-African Americans. African Americans generally work in positions that are limited in authority and scope so that they must seek approval from European Americans regarding the companies' large capital outlays.

Now, suppose that African Americans had made the choice to create businesses or to obtain jobs in African-American businesses. Then today we would have empowered African-American businesses with capital and profits sufficient to be rated as Fortune 500 companies. It is not my intention to blame certain people. We all know that past decisions were made with the best information and intentions at the time, and the past is just that: past.

My childhood education is still a part of my victim beliefs. By discussing these beliefs, however, I am in a sense changing my historical status. This allows me to know that present and future education of African-American youth must teach them, without fail, to create their own businesses and empower them to achieve a level of success second to none. The empowerment agenda requires successful African Americans to hire, train, and promote the large numbers of unemployed African-American males and females.

Academic training must be rooted in a success-oriented goal of the empowerment of African Americans. Education must be used by African Americans to build hotels, offices, homes, hospitals, automobiles; to become doctors, lawyers, farmers, machinists, truck drivers; to manufacture products, own distribution outlets, and market these products and services. African Americans need to believe, with certainty, that our success is not determined solely by European Americans.

Education can help African Americans channel our resources into institutions where we have ownership control. Education must be sought and taught with a clear purpose of empowerment.

In the past, African American children were educated around unclear ideas and goals. Consequently, the results were unclear. Today, education must be grounded in empowerment so that it has purpose and form.

Suggestions for creating New Beliefs about Education

1. Do you believe a quality education will provide you with the tools to achieve success?

2. Do you trust, respect, and admire people with high educational achievements?

3. Describe six things in life that you can acquire only with a quality education.

4. How many of these qualities do you presently possess?

5. Do you desire to possess a high level of academic achievement?

6. Reconnect with your vision of empowerment and envision yourself as a faceless, colorless, and formless being. Are you aware of the need for a quality education?

7. As a faceless, colorless, and formless being, describe the importance of education.

8. What is the role of education in guiding you to your intuitive self?

9. Can you accept yourself as being empowered without a quality education?

10. Describe education from your awareness of yourself as an empowered being.

CHAPTER FOURTEEN
VICTIM CONSCIOUSNESS

I was a victim until I envisioned myself empowered.
That's when I knew I was free

A few years ago, as I watched a movie of the life of Martin Luther King, Jr., Rev. King said something like, "I feel like sometimes I'm trying to squeeze the slave out of me." Powerful words from an insightful man. Regardless of the level of acceptance achieved in this society, the African-American male must overcome what King referred to as slave consciousness and what I call victim consciousness.

Slave consciousness and victim consciousness simply represent nonempowered thinking during different epochs. Slave consciousness is a state of mind that limits one's goals to escaping from overt physical oppression rather than moving toward empowerment. Slaves were ill equipped to fight against European Americans who used psychological and physical oppression. It is easy to imagine why they interpreted less physical oppression as a step toward empowerment rather than toward a deeper level of slave consciousness. African Americans' preoccupation with physical oppression alone has allowed the slave consciousness to govern the strategies for exercising freedom throughout the twentieth century.

During the early years of the twentieth century, African Americans were given the freedom to live in separate but unequal communities, that is, segregation. I suppose European Americans intended that African Americans maintain a slave consciousness while enjoying a semblance of power, even though that power was not transferable to the dominant society.

During the reign of segregation, a number of prominent African-American leaders such as, Booker T. Washington and W.E.B. Du Bois became spokesmen for African-American empowerment.

The common issue which interwove their philosophies was how to obtain freedom for African Americans to become a productive race within a system that had institutionalized their slave status. The exception to this approach was Marcus Garvey's "back to Africa" philosophy. Garvey believed that blacks could obtain freedom only by returning to Africa.

Many historians suggest that the philosophies of Washington and Du Bois are crucial to the strategies that African Americans developed to obtain freedom and empowerment during the past several decades. In retrospect, however, it appears to me that their philosophies promoted slave consciousness rather than empowerment. While Washington advocated blacks working for blacks and Du Bois advocated integration, both men were assimilationists. Both envisioned African Americans becoming one, in principle, with European Americans in sharing all the resources of this country.

Many African-American leaders embraced Washington's and Du Bois' vision for the empowerment of African Americans, but often were totally unaware of that vision's origin. Frustrated people sometimes long for the "good old days of segregation" as a panacea for oppression. That is because segregation created a climate for limited development of black businesses, thus giving the illusion of empowerment and control. But continually reminiscing about the good old days of segregation tends to bind us in slave/victim consciousness and diverts our energies away from empowerment.

In most instances, people long for the good old days because present conditions of oppression allow only solutions that keep them victimized. Regardless of the desires to be free, anyone born of victim consciousness remains a victim until he or she transcends the power of the senses. In contemporary America, the vision that grows out of victim consciousness moves   people   from   slavery   to   segregation,   to assimilation, and then to equality. The vision and the process are limited and are tied to a history of oppression and woundedness rooted in the general acceptance of society's perception of the African American.

At a very early age, while learning the alphabet and other facets of education, I also learned how to survive and succeed in a racially segregated world. Before becoming a victim, I was unaware of the true meaning of race consciousness. But the mind of an unvictimized African-American child is a strange phenomenon. Before the introduction of racism, a child has a vision of true empowerment. A child is unaware of the need to do great things just to become equal to another race of people. I had to be taught that whites were superior to me. When my mind would not and could not accept this idea, the white and black adults around me validated it time and time again.

When I was an unvictimized boy, adults marveled at how "smart" I was. Quite frankly, I had no idea of the true importance of being smart. I was too busy trying to convince my teachers that I had mastered what they taught me in class. I innately knew deep within that I preferred to be the student with the best grades. I preferred to be at the top rather than at the bottom or the middle of the class. Why? I really do not know and have often wondered about my classmates who were at the bottom level of the class. Did they feel "dumb" in relation to me or others who were at the top? If they felt dumb, then what dreams of success did they have for themselves?

Meanwhile, I continued to be smart as I progressed through school. At each grade level my hunger for knowledge and information increased. Without my realizing it, my indoctrination into victimhood also increased with record speed. My development, like that of millions of young people, was an essential part of an education dilemma. I was eager to learn about the world and how to participate in it. Often my eagerness to learn was in direct conflict with my intuitive knowledge. My aspirations were to fulfill those first intuitive ideas of empowerment, even though others told me I was on the wrong path. My intuitive desires for empowerment were defeated by the constant diet of ideas and philosophies leading to victimization.

When I became conscious of being a victim, about the time I graduated from high school, I developed a dislike for those who aided this process. I longed to be free from this weight of ignorance that had been placed upon me by others. I wanted to get as far away from them as possible. I wanted equality. I was now on the crowded road with millions of other African-American victims fighting to become equal to European Americans. I was screaming to the world, "I am somebody. I am equal and treat me the same as a white man."

My dreams of empowerment became visions of achieving the success that European Americans have decreed to all Americans. Success was based solely on obtaining material wealth, power, and recognition — all of which were controlled by European Americans. In a real sense, I dreamt of becoming a person who would be acceptable to European Americans. Like many others, I desired to become more like European Americans than true to my African American heritage. In my heart, I was not working to become a victim. I wanted to be an acceptable African American who could live within a system that was not designed to empower me. As a bona fide victim, my dreams of success involved obtaining a job with some status, buying a fancy car, living in a big house, and receiving recognition for my work.

All around me, I saw other African Americans fighting to change the way European Americans administered the institutions so that blacks were afforded the basic rights to eat, sleep, work, and enjoy the pursuits of happiness enjoyed by other Americans. To me, the fight for civil rights was interpreted by European Americans as a fight for acceptance and recognition rather than a fight for empowerment. However, the victim's fight is a misguided one that places him or her in conflict with his desires to be free and accepted by society, the latter of which made him a victim in the first place. Victims are incapable of developing a strategy to fight for anything. Before they can fight for freedom, they first must acknowledge that society taught them how to be a victim. Once this acknowledgment has been made, then they are capable of understanding the methods used.

Learning to become a victim is similar to learning to walk. You don't question the hollering, physical abuse and mind manipulation used by your parents to prod you along. When you begin walking, you quickly forget the methods used to help you walk. The joy of walking is sufficient by itself. Once it has been mastered, there is little need to wonder why you did not walk at three months instead of one year. This process is similar to the one a victim uses to claim his freedom by uttering the words "I am somebody" or "I am free."

The philosophy of empowerment, by definition, requires that we question not only the methods, but the effects of moving from point a to point b. What does it mean to move from living as a slave to living as a segregated Negro? Obviously, to contemporary African Americans, this question is rendered moot by the fact that neither overt slavery nor lawful racial segregation is perceived as acceptable living conditions. However, at some point in their lives, African Americans inevitably ask, "What is my purpose?" "What am I living for?" The question of purpose seems to be asked with more widespread frequency when we are feeling victimized and unempowered.

₍A victim is a person who is still tied to the European-American standards of success that act as deterrents to empowerment.₎ Regardless of his achievements, this person will view himself as someone who needs his achievements validated by European Americans. He believes that his success is inextricably tied to a four-tiered hierarchy used by whites to determine when he has made sufficient progress to assimilate into mainstream society.

The first tier represents the highest level of success in America. It can be achieved only by European-American males. This level of success is reserved for U.S. presidents, corporate executives such as Henry Ford and the Rockfellers, and heads of the leading educational, medical, publishing, and religious institutions.

The second tier is reserved for European-American males unable to achieve first tier status because of class, background, or education, European American females, and accepted African Americans, Asian Americans, and Latinos.

The third tier is reserved for the masses of poor, illiterate European-American males and females, African Americans, Asian Americans, Latinos, and Native Americans. During the physical and psychological escape from overt slavery to subtle slavery, African Americans functioned under a three-tiered system of success.

The fourth tier, which is new, is reserved for the permanent underclass: the homeless, outcast ethnic groups, and the unsuccessful. This underclass uplifts and sustains the other tiers by its presence.

Victimized African Americans aspire to be in the second or third tiers. From there they seek a separate alternate tier that they control. This alternative system is, by definition, subordinate to the European-American tier structure. That is because the success of African Americans is determined exclusively by European Americans. For example, a "truly" successful African-American athlete is one who is accepted by European Americans. Jackie Robinson was considered more successful than Satchel Paige, Larry Doby, and Josh Gibson not because he was a superior athlete, but primarily because he was the first African American to play baseball in the European-American system.

Jackie Robinson's success in the European-American tier system elevated him to the top of the African-American tier system, and he became the role model for other African-American victims. The alternate tier system created by African Americans emerged out of our collective victimization rather than our collective empowerment. It was designed to mimic success in a society that empowered European Americans and disempowered African Americans.

Nevertheless, the African-American victim seeks to join the European-American tier system. In doing so, he or she becomes an accomplice in carrying out the superiority policies of European Americans. Once a first in sports, entertainment, education, or business, is attained, the victim is satisfied and mistakes achievements for progress. For example, the victim acknowledges that Tuskegee, a black college, is academically inferior to Harvard or Yale. He ignores this belief by satisfying himself with the joy of having a black college.

Today, we must create and embody a vision of personal freedom through personal empowerment. It is a vision without victims. The European-American tier system is disintegrating and the African-American victim, for all practical purposes, died during the civil rights movement. Present and future generations will witness African Americans rejecting both the European-and African-Americans' tier systems and substituting a system of empowerment that will allow us to control our own agenda. We can squeeze the last vestiges of victimhood out of our lives and sow the seeds that will produce the harvest of our empowerment.

Suddenly Sage appeared and said, "Malcolm, an individual remains a victim whenever he gives power to his societal beliefs. As you can clearly see from examining your own beliefs, they tie you to the legacy of a victim. A victim, can never achieve empowerment without a clear understanding of the origin of these beliefs. So tell me about your spiritual beliefs."

"Gladly!" I replied. "I didn't enjoy discussing them before; they made me feel like a victim."

Suggestions for Overcoming Victim Beliefs

1. At what age did you first become aware of yourself as being powerless?

2. Describe your feelings during this moment.

3. What is your definition of a victim?

4. Do you believe a powerless person is greater than a victim?

5. Were you perceived as powerless and a victim because of your race, sex, age, etc.?

6. Reconnect with your vision of empowerment and envision yourself as a faceless, colorless, and formless being.

7. As a faceless, colorless, and formless being, do you perccive yourself as a victim?

8. From your position of empowered awareness, do you recognize the need for the existence of victims?

9. Are you now aware of being free of your victim beliefs?

10. At what moment did you stop perceiving yourself as a victim?

PART IV
METAPHYSICAL BELIEFS

CHAPTER FIFTEEN
CHRISTIANITY, RELIGION AND SPIRITUALITY

Christianity offers hope to anyone who seeks empowerment.
However, an empowered person is someone who is greater than hope.

At one point in time religion did not exist. I realize it is difficult to imagine a world existing without religion. It is not something that fell from the heavens. Religion was created by humans. According to some philosophers, humans created religion to rationalize the existence of a power greater than themselves. It was an organized attempt to unify humans with God. However, the diverse desires of human spirits made it impossible for a single religion to fulfill these desires. Consequently, the need to create Christianity, Mohammedanism, Buddhism, Hinduism, and so on.

Christianity is the religion that I was born into. To live in the United States of America and not be taught Christianity was, until very recently, to be dammed to the lower level of existence generally known as hell. Indigenous Americans were not exposed to Christianity before the European invasion; neither were Africans before slavery. So my acceptance of Christianity was an inevitable consequence of birth.

Today Christianity is still the dominant religion for most disenfranchised African Americans. Why? That is a question we must examine because true empowerment cannot be achieved until we examine the entire concept of Christianity and religion. No areas of human existence, including Christianity, are sacrosanct on the road to empowerment. All areas of life, all beliefs, and all knowledge must be carefully examined and tested to determine their usefulness to empowerment.

Since the days when my mother first introduced me to religion, I have been curious about how it could truly help anyone. My mother took me to the "holiness" church, Church of God in Christ, on Sundays. She wanted me to be "saved" from the evil doings of Satan and from going to hell when I died. Sundays, for me and millions of other African American children, were a time to learn about God and Jesus Christ.

The adults would dress in their church clothes. The minister, choir, ushers, and congregation all knew that somehow God and Jesus would be present during the church services. Once the minister and choir really reached peaks of joy, then the congregation began shouting or "getting happy" sporadically. Those who experienced these states of bliss first had to be "touched" by God, then they could enter into the hypnotic state of seemingly uncontrolled physical movements and "speak in tongues."

The people who got happy at nearly every church service were both comical and frightening to me. They were comical because it was funny to see all the grown people jumping, hollering, and acting as if they were possessed by some invisible power. They were frightening because a fist or foot might hit me in the face. I sat through years of church sermons during my childhood and was never touched by the Spirit. After years of attending church, I was so concerned that I asked my mother why I was unable to get happy during church. Her response was the same that my friends' mothers gave them, and that was: "You're too young. Once you are older and become saved, then you will be able to shout and get happy."

My friends and I, even the ones who went to other church denominations, would discuss church services in great detail to try to determine if any of us had ever felt the Spirit. We concluded at very early ages that until we became adults, the Spirit would not come to us.

Meanwhile, our Sunday school teachers taught us all about Jesus, the Bible, good living, dying, and leaving our wretched living conditions for a better place called heaven. We heard so much about heaven at the end of our physical lives that we began to disbelieve the teachings and become immune to them. I vividly recall one of my Sunday school teachers, Mr. Graves, who made quite an impression on me and my views on Christianity. He was a tall, slender man with graying hair, a Baptist deacon, and Sunday school teacher for a class of young boys. I met him after persuading my mother to let me attend the Baptist church where my friend Bobby was a member.

This Sunday school teacher was able to quote passages from the Bible with such ease that I believed he knew the true meaning of the parables Jesus taught. Mr. Graves commanded my attention as no one had done before, with the possible exception of my first grade teacher. I saw him as a righteous and God-fearing man, just like the men we studied in our Bibles. He was the person I wanted to be when I became a man.

My admiration for Mr. Graves changed one Saturday afternoon when I saw him and his friends drunk. They were cursing and staggering across the street to his house, acting just like all the other men I had seen drinking on street corners. I was so shocked, I could not believe my eyes. I felt betrayed. How could an upright Christian man do such a thing? I vowed I would never listen to him again. He was a hypocrite. I couldn't wait to tell my friends. I wanted everyone to know that he was drunk.

Mr. Graves did not attend church the next Sunday. The pastor, Rev. Amos, substituted as our teacher. For me, the class discussions were not the same without Mr. Graves. I held my pain for as long as I could, then told Rev. Amos I had something very important to discuss with him. We met later in his office and I told him that I had seen Mr.

Graves drunk. I even went so far as to say that Mr. Graves shouldn't be able to teach Sunday school anymore because he was no longer a Christian and was going to hell. I added that I didn't believe in him anymore as a servant of God.

Rev. Amos listened to me patiently until I had finished my rambling story. Then he looked directly into my eyes and said, "Let he who is without sin, cast the first stone." He added, "Mr. Graves is not God, but simply a man who is trying to live a good life. Malcolm, sometimes we place people like him on such a high pedestal that they are unable to live up to our high expectations. He needs our prayers and forgiveness."

I was glad I talked with Rev. Amos because I believed I understood what he said. Unfortunately, as a young boy, I was unable to truly understand the meaning of forgiveness. I thought forgiveness meant forgetting something had ever happened. I did just that. Mr. Graves was replaced by another teacher whom I liked just as much. I "forgave" Mr. Graves.

Meanwhile, my friends and I continued to wonder why some people were touched by the Spirit while others were not. We wanted to know why those African Americans touched by the Spirit had to live in such wretched conditions, while European Americans who prayed to the same Spirit had such power and influence over us. We never fully understood how white Christians could call our parents, relatives, and us "uncle," "auntie," "granny," "boy," and "nigger" without being punished by God. We wondered if God was on the side of the white-skinned people.

When I questioned why Jesus was white and white people had control of everything, the older blacks said: "Son, don't worry about that! Jesus is going to come back and fix everything. In the meantime, you just go ahead and do like they tell you, and one day everything will be all right."

I was learning from the adults, and I believed, as a child believes, that one day blacks would be in heaven and whites in hell. We looked for Jesus behind every face. I wondered if the Jesus we were looking for was European or African, since Jesus Christ was by definition white, at least to a majority of people. To doubt that Jesus was white was to question the authenticity of his photograph displayed in Christian churches throughout the country. No one else seemed to question Jesus' color. This was an issue to me because I was unable to identify any of us with whiteness. I also found it difficult to believe that a white man was coming back to save me from other whites.

Nonetheless, Jesus' color was never an issue for debate in the Christian church, particularly the black church. As a Christian, you were required to accept Jesus as the only "begotten son of God." This meant you also accepted his Father as white. So if you desired to be saved, you first had to accept the whiteness of Jesus. Naturally, I was confused about the entire notion of being saved.

When I asked my mother and the church leaders about the meaning of being saved, they said it meant being saved from the devil; otherwise you were unprotected from the powers of Satan. You were going to burn with Satan in eternal hell. I did not desire to burn in hell, so I became a Christian and remained a Christian throughout my childhood. Because of my fear of hell, I did not question the Christian tenets until I was much older.

In my early adult years, I became curious about the seemingly inexorable manner in which African Americans place so much trust and faith in Christianity. A major concern is the poor African Americans who adopted Christianity as the primary tool to overcome the hardships of poverty. They devoted entire lives to believing in a religion taught to them by their former owners. I wondered why anyone would trust something given to them by those who owned them as slaves. And I questioned whether there is an inherent need for humans to believe in religion.

This issue is appropriately answered by some early European philosophers who theorized that humans first believed in a divine power because they beheld with wonder the remarkable order and regularity of nature. They also theorized that the need to personify this force, to worship it, and to petition it for divine intervention led to the origin of religion.

In contrast, I believe we are born into this world knowing the causes of every event that occurs in our lives. (These causes are not concealed from us nor are we powerless to prevent unpleasant events from occurring in our lives.) From this empowered position, we are not held in a perpetual state of suspension between life and death, health and illness, employment and unemployment, love and hate, peace and turmoil. We are beyond worry and the concern of these external events and this becomes the object of our hopes and fears. My beliefs are contrary to Christianity, which teaches the opposite of intuitive knowing.

When we embrace any religious belief, we do so by acknowledging that we have lost the power to know. We separate from our true selves and lose sight of our abilities to understand what causes the events in our lives. We search for the reasons of human suffering, and seek to know why life is easier for some than others. Some people achieve riches and fame while their childhood friends remain poor. There is a tendency by some to believe that people are prosperous because they are God-fearing Christians. Thus God only rewards people who follow the Christian tenets, and to become a successful and prosperous person, we are first required to accept Christianity.

Christians have created a religion that teaches its followers to believe that God's relationship with people is similar to their relationships with government. They constantly lobby and petition God to change unpleasant things in their lives. When they are prosperous there is no need to think of the invisible author, but when they have a disastrous misfortune, God is asked to remove it. Since God is the head of the government, they must first petition God's representative for help. We ask them to pray to God for us.

Group prayer is considered one of the most powerful petitions Christians can use. Successful prayers are ones that bring immediate results. But Christianity is not the only religion that supports these beliefs. If you live in a state like California, it is important to have lots of rain. Rain helps the farmers to grow fruits and vegetables to feed people throughout the country.

A few years ago the state was in a drought. People of various religions used prayer to influence God to make it rain. They told God how unhappy they were with the drought's effects on the economy. People were losing millions of dollars, lawns were dying, and water was not served with restaurant meals. They told God that life would be better with rain. Needless to say, their prayers did not result in substantial rain for several years.

Ministers on radio and television throughout the country pray to God to help all the people who are sick, troubled, worried, poor, and victims of crime and drugs. Some offer their listeners better results if they send the ministers financial donations. The larger the donation, the greater the results. The ministers claim that the church and God are happy with people who give money freely and joyously. However, most people are never satisfied with this arrangement for very long. The prayers that are continually offered to God prove they are not all satisfied with God's administration.

According to American Christians, God is embodied in spirit in the church. The church is the organization that spreads the Christian doctrine, assists lost souls with achieving salvation, and monitors the evil ways of humans. The church, by Christian definition, is sacrosanct. Another definition, however, of the church may be that it legitimizes the wretched living conditions of many in society by offering believers hope for a better life in Heaven.

The church has a history of offering salvation to all who are "troubled and heavy laden." It addresses the needs of some people better than others. The church's goal is to be the organization that empowers people to have freedom and peace. However, in the case of blacks, the church has been unable to use its influence to provide them with freedom or peace. In fact, Christianity legitimized slavery in American. It justified and explained racism as being sanctioned by God. Christianity was introduced to the slaves as a religion that gave God's power to whites. Blacks were believed to be without souls and therefore incapable of acquiring empowerment.

The Christian church's role in American society is to be a part of it, support it, and provide a moral basis for its policies. Unfortunately, many African Americans believe the church should question unjust laws, advocate changes, and provide leadership for its powerless citizens. Within this context they have used Christianity to mobilize blacks to limited action. However, they were afraid to use Christianity to challenge the overall system for fear of being labeled communist or anti-American.

Christianity offers blacks spiritual sovereignty to express and enjoy human freedom in another world. When they complain of evils, Christianity refers them to Heaven for the solutions. They are told that when they reach the other world, God will repair all the iniquities and miseries that he permits to exist on earth for a short time. Neither African Americans, nor any other disenfranchised people, however, are likely to be impressed for long with a religion that asks them to not hope for any improvement, that assures them it is a waste of time to try to make conditions better and that they must remain content to endure war, exploitation, misery, and injustice on this earth.

It will not satisfy contemporary African Americans to be told that there is ultimate compensation for them and their children in another world beyond relative time. Most humans are primarily concerned with enjoying prosperity within their lifetimes. I believe religion is viable for oppressed people when it concerns this world and its living conditions. When religion focuses on rewards in another world, it has, in fact, lost its ability to empower African Americans.

Hard times, misinformation, and a hunger for empowerment cause African Americans to seek solace outside of themselves. They seek a deliverer at every turn of despair and hopelessness. Nearly all religious doctrine, especially Christianity, reveals prophecies of saviors, messiahs, and redeemers coming from heaven. Christianity has had a long-standing prophccy that a divine deliverer would descend from heaven, relieve the world from its depressed state, and ameliorate conditions so that people can live in a state of permanent happiness.

A serious question arises from the Christian beliefs in messiahs and deliverers: do African Americans conceive of the Messiah as a white or black man? This question is important because most blacks are taught that Jesus is white, and therefore the coming Messiah will be white. Blacks are taught to perceive black leaders as Moses, but not as the Messiah. And while Moses is believed to be close to God, he was not "his only begotten son." Perhaps this point is best illustrated by sharing with you a television interview of a black Christian minister.

As a lifelong Christian who believed that Jesus is God's only begotten son, this minister strongly opposed displaying the picture of a white Jesus in black churches. He discussed his decision to replace that picture with one of a black Jesus. He argued, "There was more than ample historical data to support the claim that Jesus was black. Most of the people who lived in the part of the world where Jesus lived were dark-skinned. The attempts by white Christians to give Jesus European characteristics of blue eyes and blond hair were designed to empower all people who look liked that." He continued, "Blacks can not feel a sense of identification with a white Jesus since whites are the people blamed for most of their suffering in this country." "Blacks," he said, "need to have a black face as the mediator between God and humans."

I listened to him with great interest because his explanations seemed to be compatible with the views of a growing number of African-American ministers. But further into his discussion he said, "Even though I have a picture of a black Jesus in my church, it is impossible for me to remove the image of the white Jesus from my mind. However, I believe that by displaying the black Jesus to young African-American children, they will be able to see themselves empowered in blackness rather than as victims in whiteness."

The minister's words had broken part of the chain of Christian slavery. He addressed the question of whether the Messiah was a black or white man. The entire notion of a messiah is a necessary ingredient for many religions. I am told by other students of religion that while there are many similarities between Jesus and Mohammed, neither faith — Christianity and Mohammedanism — is able to accept the tenets of the other and remain the true way to God. Christians accept the philosophy of Jesus as the sole representative of God. Muslims accept the philosophy of Mohammed as representing the sole desires of God (Allah).

The belief of a messiah has created a popular theory among African Americans that Christianity will produce the Messiah. In this regard, an inordinate number of African American leaders have used the church as the base to fight against the injustices perpetrated on African Americans. To become a successful African-American leader, it helped to be a Christian, especially a Protestant minister. It was difficult to be an African-American leader without receiving a call from God first.

Today, there are literally thousands of ministers propagating a limited doctrine of empowerment through the church. For many on the road to empowerment, blind acceptance of Christianity by purpose, definition, and deed becomes a stumbling block. This is partly due to the fear that an omnipotent and omniscient God would create inferior human beings into a world of seemingly never-ending sin.

Nevertheless, as one who has been raised as a victim, and who has embraced Christianity as my salvation, I am still free to use my thoughts and observations of world events. I am, however, a prisoner of Christianity as long as I believe it is the way to freedom. I can reject its power as easily as I rejected the beliefs that Columbus discovered America and Jesus was white.

The freedom to seek empowerment comes when the desire to be free overshadows the desire to be enslaved. Empowerment is a consciousness that transcends Christianity and religion. Empowered consciousness is the state of awareness obtainable by every individual, literate or illiterate, when the will to question becomes an effortless habit.

Suggestions for Creating Empowered Beliefs of Spirituality

1. When did you first become aware of religion?

2. Describe your initial feelings regarding religion.

3. What association did you form between religion and God?

4. Did you believe that religion provided you with the tools to communicate with God?

5. What were some of the fears you acquired from your religious beliefs?

6. What were some of the powers you acquired from your religious beliefs?

7. Reconnect with your vision of empowerment and envision yourself as a faceless, colorless, and formless being. In this state of awareness, are you in need of religion?

8. As a faceless, colorless, and formless being, describe religion within the context of your vision.

9. Describe the relationship between your spiritual awareness of empowerment and your awareness of religion.

10. From a position of empowered awareness, can you accept yourself as a spiritual being who is free of religious beliefs?

CHAPTER SIXTEEN
TRANSFORMATION

Set your sights on the vision and think of nothing else.
Relax your consciousness to act in the present and when your
vision is manifested into the world, it will be you who the world sees.

Today my thoughts are beyond the memories of a six year old boy. Today I stand at the door of empowerment. I knock and the door opens. I enter into a new state of awareness that reveals my intuitive thoughts standing on the illusions of lack, limitation, and struggle. Suddenly, I realize that to become the person I see, I must accept myself in this new form. A closer look reveals that beneath me is the glowing image of the victim, Malcolm Kelly. Strangely, I clearly see the differences between my empowered and my victimized thoughts. Now I must decide between the two. It helps to recall the vivid conversation I had with Sage about standing in my truth. I want to share my recollection of that conversation with you.

Sage stared at me seriously and said, "Malcolm, you have spent a considerable amount of time on the empowerment road reflecting on your life and the lives of other African Americans. I don't know why, but I suspect that you have not told me the true reason you got off the crowded road."

I paused for a few moments. "Yes, my wise old friend," I replied with a smile, "you are so correct. I got off the crowded road not solely because I was curious about the people living by the side of the road. I got off to find my place in a world that seemed unwilling to address the spiritual visions of African Americans who, for many reasons, are unable to achieve self-empowerment. Sage, it is not an easy task to live in the physical body of an African American in a country designed to fulfill the aspirations of European Americans at our expense."

Sage stood, bowed his head, placed his hands behind him, and asked, "Malcolm, the subjects you discuss in this book are sufficient, if understood and practiced, to start other American Americans on the process of self-empowerment. Is your inner truth also the truth about the world? Or is the outside world the truth about you?"

"Sage! That's a tough question," I replied with a nervous chuckle. "Let me try to answer you this way. When I first met you and began to discuss these complex issues, I believed that once I mastered these subjects I would become empowered. Once I began, however, I realized they were all leading me to the ultimate challenge: using all the principles of empowerment. To do so I first had to embody clarity of purpose, courage, and integrity, as well as freedom of fear, worry, doubt, and loneliness. My embodiment of empowerment consciousness represented the key steps I had to take before using the principles of empowerment."

"Very good, Malcolm," he interrupted with an expression of approval. "I'm pleased to see that you have gained considerable insight into your intuitive self in such a short time."

"Thank you, Sage! I needed to hear you say that," I replied with my arms extended in a gesture of gratitude. "I've shared recollections of my life within the context of empowerment so that others may become stimulated to examine their lives, too. I discovered, however, that sharing my experiences with strangers is a new, difficult, and yet freeing experience.

"Frequently I regret ever talking about the subject of empowerment. During these moments, I constantly worry that I am unworthy to claim ownership of my intuitive consciousness. In fact I've asked others not to embrace empowerment as merely another psychological fad to make people feel good about themselves. I warned them to pursue empowerment with caution."

Sage looked at me somewhat perplexed. "Malcolm, why do you make such a request?" he asked. "I have listened to you discuss the complex questions raised by all victims, and I am confident that you have benefited from the discussions. By using the principles you are in a position to mover farther down the road. The early part of the journey causes victims to perceive themselves as vulnerable, lonely, and insecure. Every decision you make during this early period causes intense human pain. The pain may be so intense that you begin to question why anyone would give up their position in society just to try and find out what's troubling their hearts) The truth you seek is located within intuitive consciousness. It is always present."

"I believe you," I responded, nodding my head in agreement. "But it's very difficult to accept invisible ideas as reality. You know, it's difficult to stand in your truth solely on the basis of intuition."

"Believe me, Malcolm, I understand you," he replied with a smile. "Many years ago, I talked with several other African Americans who got off the crowded road of life and traveled down the road to empowerment. After they bared their hearts about how one becomes a victim of human ignorance, they, too, felt the need to stand in their truth and use the principles. And as you will find out soon, to use the principles effectively, you must use empowerment techniques every minute of every hour of every day until they become as much a part of you as blinking your eyes)That is, they become effortless habits.

"Malcolm, even now as you travel farther you will encounter many experiences designed to either empower or send you back to the crowded road. Your mind and intellect will pressure you to accept reason instead of empowerment. Your friends' positions in society will make you feel a twinge of envy and jealousy because it will appear that failure accompanies all your acts to obtain empowerment. There will be many days when you desire to feel the warmth of crowds.

Empowerment will begin to seem like a bad dream. As you become stronger, the victim in you will intensify its power and cause you to doubt yourself."

"I don't know how you know it, but that's exactly what happened to me," I interrupted. "I mean, I felt so badly that I really wanted to return to the crowded road."

"Malcolm, when you feel a lack of self-confidence in your decisions, remember you are merely moving further away from the control of your nonempowered self. You are on the journey home. And, like a child separated from his or her parents, it is natural to be afraid of darkness and being alone. But remember, darkness is a thing found only in the victim part of you. To find the way to the light of intuition you must travel far away from darkness."

I nodded my head in agreement. "I know what you are saying is so true because a few months ago, when I first spoke from my heart about empowerment, I began to see many different things that caused me to question my status in the world. It seemed the more fervently I talked to African Americans about empowerment, the more I came face to face with the appearances of failure and doubt. They challenged my commitment to the principles. These situations were so real and powerful that they caused me to temporarily abandon the principles and revisit my past habits of worry, fear, anger, envy, loneliness, deprivation, and the inability to perceive limitless opportunities. Here's what happened!

"Several years ago, my wife and I started a personnel business and like so many other people who start businesses, we were unable to obtain unsecured credit. Like others, we used our house as collateral to obtain a bank loan. And like most entrepreneurs, we put our beliefs in the success of the business above everything else."

"That was a brave thing to do," Sage interrupted with a

complimentary expression of approval. "Most victims are afraid to risk their savings on an iffy thing such as a new business venture."

"I hear you," I responded with a smile. "In our case, our beliefs in the success of the business were in a constant state of flux, vacillating between rational and intuitive consciousness. Unfortunately, when you do business with a bank, the bank listens and responds only to things rooted in rational consciousness: facts, facts, and more facts. Bank officials are trained to ignore anything rooted in intuitive consciousness. So most entrepreneurs whose business ideas are formed from intuitive consciousness are forced to use logic to communicate with banks. If not, they are placed in a position to feel even more like a victim. Do you understand what I'm saying?"

"Yes, I understand you quite well," he replied in a barely audible voice. "Please don't interpret my silence as a lack of interest. I want you to keep talking so that you can hear the words of a victim pleading for help."

"Anyway, as I was saying, banks do business with already successful businesses," I continued. "If you have good clients, impressive receivables, financial management systems, and a documented success in the field, you are in a position to discuss loans. Some small business people believe that banks only give you a loan when you don't need it. Before obtaining the bank loan, we had already established a successful client list."

"That's good, Malcolm," he interrupted and shook his head in agreement. "I mean, you should feel proud of your accomplishments."

"Yeah, I guess that was pretty good, huh!" I responded with a loud laugh. "You know, sometimes you overlook the good things you're doing because you're so upset with the bad things. Well, most of our clients were major corporations. We were in the process of expanding our business to cover a larger geographical area. In order to grow, we needed access to capital. Anyway, to make a long story short, we obtained the loan from the bank; although it was not nearly the amount we needed, it was a start."

"Malcolm, when you're beginning a journey, whether it's business or empowerment, the first part of the journey is always the most difficult," Sage said instructively. "The first decisions lay the foundation for the other levels of growth. If they are not wise decisions, then expect the rest of the journey to be shaky."

"Yeah, I wish I had known then what I know now," I said. "We grew very quickly by acquiring office space in class A buildings in the three largest cities in the San Francisco Bay Area. We employed several hundred temporary and permanent employees, 90 ninety percent African Americans. We were one of the largest African-American-owned businesses in our field in the state. We developed a reputation for providing our clients with quality services. Man, I felt empowered every time I came into my office and saw all the nice furniture, equipment, and the professional African-American staff. I had arrived!"

"I'm sure it made you feel good," he replied with his arms in an open gesture of freedom. "But, you need to ask yourself: What did you learn from this?"

"Sage, I learned that we were unprepared to meet all the challenges associated with rapid growth. Just look at poor athletes and entertainers who obtained riches quickly. We began to experience collection problems with our clients. Within a few months, we were unable to collect on the receivables in time to pay the loan. After several failures, the bank arbitrarily gave us a 30-day demand payment letter.

"Several months later, even after I made numerous requests for forbearance, the bank foreclosed on my business accounts and my home that was collateral. In a matter of a few months I went from earning revenues of over $100,000 per month to $8,000 per month. For all practical purposes, I was out of business."

"What were your feelings when this happened?" he asked with a curious facial expression. "Did you feel like a failure?"

"Yeah, I did," I answered with regret and anger. "The difficulty with accepting myself as a failure is that I gave power to the events unfolding around me, and that determined the actions I took. When I believed that I was going out of business, I planned to go out of business, rather than planned to expand the business.

"Man, when I had to disengage from some of my material possessions and perceived status, I wanted very badly to remain a nonempowered thinking man."

"Your feelings were similar to the ones most victims have when they act to leave the crowded road," he interrupted. "Change causes victims to try to stay put."

"I felt that way, too," I said with a smile. "In my heart, at least during the early stages when I worried about losing these possessions, I wanted to keep everything — business, home, and everything else — exactly as it was. I wanted to go to the next level, but I wanted everything to go intact with me. It was during this period of selfishness that my intellect once again tried to control my consciousness."

"Intuition creates some strange experiences for neophytes," Sage interrupted with a laugh. "It keeps you from become overconfident with yourself."

"Well," I replied, "I found that my intellect, which I had previously cherished above everything else, used its power to create doubt about the correct decision that would lead me to the next level of consciousness. Doubt, the essence of a victim's beliefs, would not allow me to get any advice that didn't support the conclusion that I was losing and failing, rather than gaining and succeeding.

"My intellect told me my situation was logically hopeless and advised me to accept that I tried hard to succeed, but things just didn't work out for me. I should just move on and make sure I never make this mistake again. The intellect said it would place a file in my rational consciousness to ensure that in the future I would be more cautious in taking risks based on ideas coming from the intuitive consciousness. 'Don't worry, I won't let anything like this happen to you again,' rational consciousness said."

"Malcolm, doubt is the most powerful of all victim beliefs," Sage interrupted, pointing his finger. "Whenever victims encounter doubt, they automatically turn to rational ideas for solutions."

"Regrettably, I must agree with you," I said. "We have been conditioned by our experiences to rely on logic and reason as the best tools for solving problems. Our entire learning process is based on acquiring layers and layers of information about how to logically solve problems when confronted with a difficult situation."

"Unfortunately, you are correct," Sage said. "These are the layers of ignorance that keeps you as a victim. Please continue."

"A good example of what I'm saying is this," I continued. "When the leader of a country is faced with a major problem such as war or an economic recession, he or she seeks advice from experts. Each advisor gives the leader logical options on what should and should not be done to solve this problem. The leader normally accepts this advice and makes a decision. However, we know that some leaders reject their advisors' advice and follow their gut feelings. When they rely on intuition, their advisors marvel at their courage, conviction, and strength to make difficult decisions.

"Most of us who are faced with less difficult problems, pay for counsel from doctors, lawyers, accountants, or people who have acquired knowledge in the area of our concern. Very rarely would a victim seek advice on how to start a business from someone who has never owned or operated one. We have been taught to accept expert information. Even highly educated victims will not deviate from what they were first taught. Doctors always follow the surgical procedures they learned in medical school. The same thing applies to a general fighting a war. Victims accept advice given by the experts in their fields."

"I agree with you," Sage replied. "That's why they remain as victims. Invariably, victims succumb to the illusions and self-doubts of the images around them. Do you agree?"

"Absolutely!" I answered. "When confronted with the external appearances, the illusions of losing and failing, I immediately became a victim of rational consciousness. I initially couldn't find the power, will, or confidence to trust my intuition. So I sought advice from outside experts. I was still uncomfortable using intuition as the basis for making important decisions about my life.

"Unfortunately, I let victim beliefs provide me with a solution for losing and failing. I reacted out of habit and used the powers of worry, fear, doubt, and anger to make decisions, trying to move from hopelessness to contentment. It seemed that just as quickly as I thought I had left those beliefs behind, I was now, by habit, falling into their web again. And each kept me thinking that there were no answers beyond logic, except ignorance."

"Did you find your victim experiences and beliefs adequate to solve your problems?" he interrupted.

"Yes! I believed that my experiences and victim beliefs could have solved the problem," I responded, with disbelief at my quick answer. "However, this required me to reject the principles of empowerment and remain a victim. My business attorney, who was a nonempowered man, suggested that I use law, the techniques of society.

These laws, he said, allow people another chance to rebuild their lives through trial and error."

"In other words, he suggested that you file for bankruptcy," Sage interrupted in a matter-of-fact tone. "It's okay for you to say it now; it's the only way you will ever remove the stigma of failure from your beliefs."

"You can see that I was hesitant to tell you about my bankruptcy," I replied with a nervous smile. "Well, it's true. I really didn't want anyone, especially my friends, to know about it. You see, when my wife and I came face to face with losing our business and home, we firmly believed this represented failure. We accepted the appearance of losing; we became incapable or unwilling to perceive it as temporary. (Society taught us to accept temporary set-backs as failures) At any time when many of the things we loved were taken from us, we relied on doubt, fear, worry, and anger to help us overcome the loss."

"It's sad, isn't it, that victims find it difficult to publicly express the pain in their lives," he interrupted, rubbing his hand through his hair.

"You know, Sage," I replied, "to involuntarily give up something that you desire to keep is considered by society to be a loss. In other words, nonempowered rationality is determined by your desire to claim things such as houses, cars, family, clothes, and job as your essence. Once I reacted to my situation from fear, worry, doubt, and anger, I automatically gave my power to the bank. Whenever you give away your power, then you're a victim.

"So, thinking like a powerless victim, I imagined that the bank would plaster a large sign on my front door alerting neighbors and everyone else that our home was being foreclosed and sold at a public auction. I couldn't perceive anything worse than that. "You see, the powers of worry now extended their tentacles to the bank. The more I worried and acted out of fear, the more I became a victim of rational thinking."

"Malcolm, unfortunately what you did confirmed your victim beliefs," he interrupted. "By returning to your victim comfort zone of worry, fear, and self-doubt, you placed your trust in a belief system fraught with struggle and confusion. Consequently, you failed to see the true meaning of your actions, only the fast-growing illusions of failure."

"I hate to admit it," I said, "but I didn't know what else to do, except worry about what I believed was about to happen to me. I realize that some people who read about this may have experienced a similar situation in their lives. Others, not having experienced such an event, may find it incredulous that a successful person like me would allow a bank foreclosure to happen. Surely they would ask, 'Couldn't you have done something to prevent it? Were you naive or stupid?'

"In retrospect, I might have made different decisions that may or may not have prevented this predicament. But I am also cognizant that the policies that banks use when doing business with blacks are different from the policies established for whites. Just look at the number of banks who have admitted these differences by committing billions of dollars to the Community Reinvestment Act. However, I am still grateful that the Creator and my intuitive consciousness gave me the opportunity to experience true empowerment. If the bank had not treated me so harshly, I would not have written this book."

"Oh, I don't know about that," Sage interrupted. "I'm confident that you were created to write this book as part of a greater purpose. And if it hadn't been the bank, then it would have been something else. The incidence with the bank occurred when you were ready to change and seek the meaning of empowerment."

"I suppose you're right," I replied with a chuckle. "Ultimately, the bank's actions forced me to rely on the truth of my other self — my intuition, or that part of me that precedes and is greater than intellect. That part of me is capable, if allowed, of making perfect decisions. Though some people ruled by the intellect may refer to it as gut feelings, intuitive decision-making is a different form of human reasoning. It is the part of you and me that is constantly, without fail, connected to the Creator of the universe — the cause of everything seen and unseen.

"Anyway," I continued, "when I stood in my truth and trusted my intuitive self, I was no longer engulfed by doubt, worry, and fear. I was now trusting the accurateness of decisions made outside of intellect. But I must confess, it was difficult for me to abandon rational thinking for intuitive thinking. (Leaving the world of mathematics, science, logic, and language, and using intuitive consciousness required that I assemble a new data base) For me to stand in the face of crisis and embrace empowerment required that I subordinate my longtime guide, the intellect. I quickly discovered that whenever you use the principles of empowerment, you must relinquish rational beliefs, and previous accomplishments, and embark on a new, less traveled path of "learning — the path of empowerment. It is a difficult task for those who love and trust rational beliefs."

Sage smiled and said, "It's difficult, but not impossible. The pain is caused by the rebirth process, not from the use of the principles."

I shook my head and said, "I agree with you. Using the principles of empowerment initially caused pain. (The pain comes primarily when one is separated from one's self.) It's the part of the self left behind, unhappy and unwilling to accept the separation. However, the one who endures the pain and seeks the secrets of empowerment is rewarded by understanding that he or she existed before the creation of language and its expression of the world.

"You know, Sage," I continued, "the good thing about using the principles is that I didn't stop when the appearances of failure grew in power. I used the principles to remove them so I could work to bring my vision of empowerment into the world. When I focused on my vision, the fears and worry gave way to courage and determination. And within a twelve-month period, I had more clients. I had expanded my business services and moved into a house almost twice as large and expensive as the other one.

"I now use the principles of empowerment daily to guide me through the problems created by my interpretation of the events in my life. I know that when you use the principles, nothing is removed from your life without being replaced by something else. We must not judge the appearances of the gift, but accept it as one accepts the body's ability to process food."

"Also, Malcolm," Sage interrupted, "I want you to remember that the principles of empowerment are not bound by human time. One can go 'up' faster than one goes 'down.' So whenever a thing is removed from your life, you should recognize it as something that had been borrowed, for a short time, like one's body. None of the things created by nonempowered consciousness is permanent. We can only own our intuitive-consciousness self."

"Unfortunately, Sage, I had to learn this the hard way," I replied with a smile. "Sometimes, like today, when I reflect on my life's learning and decisions, I constantly refer to a time after the creation of language, rather than a time before its creation. I try to remember the differences between relevant and absolute time. Relevant time, intellect, is rooted primarily in the birth of the body, while absolute time, intuition, is rooted in eternal creation. When I forget the differences between the two, my problems become more difficult to solve. Whenever this happens, I have to go far enough away from the problems to reach a point where I am worry free.

"You know, as African Americans, we measure our accomplishments in a slave/master historical context and, consequently, we are victims with a limited perspective of the truth about our creation. By using intuitive consciousness to sift through the layers of intellectual experiences, we find the truth about ourselves."

Sage sat down and poured a glass of water. He looked at it and then said, "Malcolm, I know the real truth of the universe and I know that empowerment will guide and keep you and others on the road to these same truths. I also know that if you travel farther on the road without sharing your experiences with using the principles, you will limit your ability to effectively communicate with the lovers of rational beliefs.

"Many years ago, when I first began to use the principles of empowerment, I realized that I was totally free from nonempowered consciousness. I knew the true relationship between humans and their things, that is, houses, cars, money, jobs, businesses, power, and so on. But when I communicated with people about their temporal relationship with things, many felt I was not rational. And to be described as not rational by humans meant I was not believable."

"I find that interesting," I said. "I never expected to hear you say something like this. I mean, you seem to have it together and everything."

"Malcolm, whenever I spoke about using consciousness to change the appearance of one thing for another, I met resistance. Whenever I told people that intuitive consciousness is free of restrictions and available to anyone according to one's power to use it, I met resistance. However, whenever I told them that material wealth could be had through a good education, hard work, an understanding of the democratic system, and positive thinking, I met no resistance."

"Unfortunately, Sage, that's pretty much all we want to hear," I interrupted. "I mean, the basic objective of all victims is to accumulate material possessions."

"Malcolm, that's why I'm concerned if you continue farther on the road, the vast amount of information given to you might be too much for you to communicate to others. Your acquisition of the knowledge of intuitive consciousness will cause people who are locked into rational thinking to perceive you as an anomaly to human development. They will think you have some hidden secrets to empowerment without realizing that they, too, can use the same principles without any assistance from you.

"So I strongly advise you to tell anyone who seeks empowerment about your experiences. (Ask them to join you on the road to empowerment.) Share with them your understanding of empowerment. Remind them of their existence in a time and place when they were free to create and express an infinite number of life expressions."

"I agree with you," I said. "Now that I know how to make it to this point on the road, I feel confident that I can return here again. There is one question I must ask you before I go: Will you be here when I return?"

"Malcolm, for you to ask me that question is to restore your nonempowered self to power," he replied with a look of impatience. "You and I, and all others, obtain our power from the same source. We knew each other before the things of the world existed. When we embody the principles of empowerment, we become guides who lead. We use the less-traveled road — the road that leads to true empowerment. Intellect cannot read the empowerment maps. Without intuitive maps, one merely travels in uncharted darkness.

"So Malcolm," he continued, "you and all humans already have the intuitive maps to guide you through worry, fear, and loneliness. It is your responsibility to share the maps with anyone who requests them as a guide to their own intuitive consciousness.

"Remember, you and all others who seek the knowledge of empowerment have within you the power to create ideas and transform them into things not yet present in the world. So continue to use your intuitive consciousness. Very soon you will see the limitless results you get from this source of power."

I opened my eyes and he was gone. I suddenly realized that I was beyond the grasp of anger, fear, worry, self-hatred, racism, and doubts. I smiled and acknowledged my birth as "The New African American Man."

more - less
authenticity
Dysfunctional = choose to do same.
Uniqueness to yourself = life purpose --
Difficult to let go of your life investment
Solitary profession :
5 years
changing inward hard
Most people live to mediocrity
I can't do kills vision
Take invisible idea and bring it into world.
Get into practice of trusting yourself
Worry, fear, doubt are manifestation of
                                        powerlessness
Faith lead u to power
"took the time, took the action"

    O Let There Be Life --
            Teacher
    Spiritual Opportunities
    { Contract of life }= } mental
      Expert advice } }   engram
                      plenty of love, abundance,